Short Stories
for Creative Language Classrooms

Short Stories
for Creative Language Classrooms

**Joanne Collie
and Stephen Slater**

CAMBRIDGE UNIVERSITY PRESS
Cambridge, New York, Melbourne, Madrid, Cape Town, Singapore, São Paulo

Cambridge University Press
The Edinburgh Building, Cambridge CB2 2RU, UK

www.cambridge.org
Information on this title: www.cambridge.org/9780521406536

© Cambridge University Press 1993

This publication is in copyright. Subject to statutory exception
and to the provisions of relevant collective licensing agreements,
no reproduction of any part may take place without the written
permission of Cambridge University Press.

First published 1993
10th printing 2006

Printed in the United Kingdom at the University Press, Cambridge

A catalogue record for this publication is available from the British Library

ISBN-13 978-0-521-40653-6 paperback
ISBN-10 0-521-40653-6 paperback

ISBN-13 978-0-521-40652-9 cassette
ISBN-10 0-521-40652-8 cassette

Contents

Stories		Themes
To the learner	1	
Stories		**Themes**
The star by Alasdair Gray	3	Escape from routine – Loneliness The rich world of the imagination
Strange animal an African story re-told by Alexander McCall Smith	9	Tolerance of others – The magic of music Family relationships
Hannah by Malachi Whitaker	15	Youthful anticipation – Social conventions Unexpected turns in life – Regrets
Report on the shadow industry by Peter Carey	21	Reality and illusion – Escapism The search for happiness
Verbal transcription – 6 a.m. by William Carlos Williams	33	Everyday concerns in crisis situations Behaviour in emergencies
The debutante by Leonora Carrington	38	Cruelty beneath civilised behaviour Reality and dream
Important things by Barbara L. Greenberg	47	Parents and children What is important in life?
Secrets by Tim Winton	52	A child's vision of the adult world Family breakdown and the need for love
Dazzler by Suniti Namjoshi	60	Introverts and extroverts Different ways of solving problems
Misunderstood an anonymous story	65	Animals and humans The importance of communication
Shell songs A letter from the Laird's wife by George Mackay Brown	73	Rich and poor Intuition versus the intellect People and nature

The authors of the stories	83
Notes on the stories	85
Key	92
Tapescripts	94
To the teacher	97
Bibliography	101

Acknowledgements

The authors would like to thank Peter Donovan, James Dingle and Joanne Currie of Cambridge University Press, and also Angela Wilde, Annie Cornford and Barbara Thomas for their help.

The authors and publishers are grateful to the following copyright owners for permission to reproduce copyright material. Every endeavour has been made to contact copyright owners and apologies are expressed for any omissions.

Canongate Press plc for 'The star' and 'Strange animal'.   Carcanet Press Limited for 'Hannah'.   Rodgers, Coleridge & White Ltd. and the University of Queensland Press for 'Report on the shadow industry', from *The Fat Man in History* by Peter Carey, University of Queensland Press, 1974. © Peter Carey, 1974.   New Directions Publishing Corporation for 'Verbal transcription – 6 a.m'. © William Carlos Williams, 1950.   Virago Press for 'The debutante'. © Editions Flammarion, 1978.   Barbara L. Greenberg for 'Important things'. © Barbara L. Greenberg.   Tim Winton for 'Secrets'. © Tim Winton, 1983. Suniti Namjoshi for 'Dazzler'. © Suniti Namjoshi.   Collins, an imprint of HarperCollins Publishers Limited for 'Shell songs'.

The authors and publishers are grateful to the following illustrators and photographic sources.

Illustrators: Peter Byatt: pp. 19, 47, 71.   Helen Humphreys: pp. 3, 9, 12, 21, 31, 33, 51, 62, 80.   Nigel Paige: p. 37.   Tony Watson: p. 2.   Rosemary Woods: p. 26.

Cover illustration by Rosemary Woods.

Photographic sources: p.11: Jafta Cards, Harare, Zimbabwe.   p. 38 (top left): *War and Corpses – Last Hope of the Rich*, 1932 by John Heartfield. Supplied by the Archiv Für Kunst und Geschichte Berlin. © DACS 1993.   p. 38 (top right): *Perpetual Motion* by René Magritte. Private collection. Supplied by The Bridgeman Art Library, London. © ADAGP, Paris and DACS, London 1993.   p. 38 (bottom left): *Through Birds Through Fire But Not Through Glass*, 1943 by Yves Tanguy. Minneapolis Society of Fine Arts, Minnesota. Supplied by The Bridgeman Art Library, London. © DACS 1993.   p. 38 (bottom right): *Bird Pong*, 1949 by Leonora Carrington. Ex-Edward James Foundation, Sussex. Supplied by The Bridgeman Art Library, London. © 1992 Leonora Carrington / ARS, New York. p.44: Ronald Sheridan, The Ancient Art and Architecture Collection.   p. 46: *Self Portrait 1936–7* by Leonora Carrington. Supplied by The Serpentine Gallery, London. © 1992 Leonora Carrington / ARS, New York.

To the learner

Reading a good book in our own language is usually an enjoyable experience. Sitting in our armchair, we float away into the totally different world of the book – a world that is sometimes unpredictable, strange and exciting. In this world, however, we can recognise situations that are like ours at home and people who think and act like us. Quite often we feel as though we are actually living in that world. The people we meet in its pages become as familiar as friends.

Reading a good story in a language that is not our own can be like that too, even though it is a bit more of a challenge. It is our hope that you will find the stories in this book interesting and rewarding – worth the effort of getting to know them.

You will probably be reading these stories in a classroom first, rather than in your own armchair. Working with other people in groups gives you a lot of advantages: you can help each other with difficulties, and you can share ideas, reactions, and interpretations. The classroom situation gives you a chance to talk about what you have read and to compare ideas, because everyone is exploring the same story. Of course, you can carry on talking about a text after the class, over a cup of coffee or a bite to eat.

On the other hand, you also need some time by yourself with a story. You will want to make your own relationship with it. So after you have read or heard stories in class and worked with them in groups, you might like to re-read them on your own. The cassette lets you listen as you read, if you prefer to do that.

In re-reading these stories we are sure you will understand aspects that were not so clear before. Don't worry too much if there are words you don't understand, especially at first – quite often the meaning will become clear as you talk about a story in class or re-read it at home. Whether you read stories in your own language or in another language, you can get a lot from a rich or complex work even if at the end there are still aspects that remain puzzling.

These stories have not been simplified or abridged for you. They are not extracts but complete short stories. Some of the longer ones have been broken up into smaller parts so that you can read them first in more manageable 'chunks' if you or your teacher choose to.

Each story offers different *creative development* activities to choose from. Sometimes these take you back to the text to extend your understanding of it, sometimes they take you into a parallel situation or a creative one.

To the learner

You are not expected to do them all, but to choose those that seem most interesting. This is the opportunity to express your own ideas, and to find out what others in your class think or feel.

We have tried to give you a selection of stories that are varied and come from different parts of the world. We hope that you will discover two kinds of pleasure in becoming familiar with them – finding out how different people are, and finding out how alike, in some ways, we all are.

Happy reading!

Joanne Collie

Stephen Slater

The star

by Alasdair Gray

A What thoughts go through your mind when you gaze up at the star-filled sky on a clear night? Look at the star and then talk about your experiences with someone else in the class.

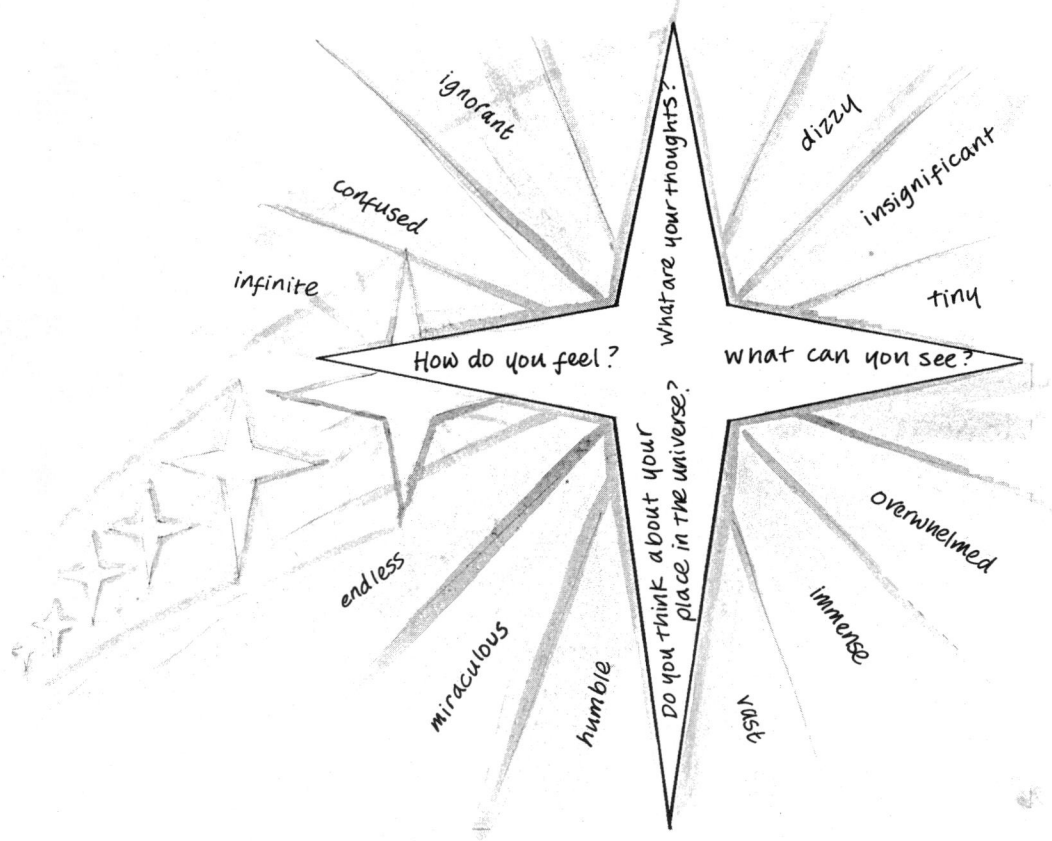

B Here are the first and last sentences of this short story. What could it be about? Together, discuss various possibilities.

First sentence of the story:

A star had fallen beyond the horizon, in Canada perhaps.

Last sentence of the story:

Teacher, classroom, world receded like a rocket into a warm, easy blackness leaving behind a trail of glorious stars, and he was one of them.

The star

Read the story for the first time and listen to it on the cassette.

A star had fallen beyond the horizon, in Canada perhaps. (He had an aunt in Canada.) The second was nearer, just beyond the iron works, so he was not surprised when the third fell into the backyard. A flash of gold light lit the walls of the enclosing tenements and he heard a low musical chord. The light turned deep red and went out, and he knew that somewhere below a star was cooling in the night air. Turning from the window he saw that no-one else had noticed. At the table his father, thoughtfully frowning, filled in a football coupon, his mother continued ironing under the pulley with its row of underwear. He said in a small voice, 'A'm gawn out.'

His mother said, 'See you're no' long then.'

He slipped through the lobby and onto the stairhead, banging the door after him.

The stairs were cold and coldly lit at each landing by a weak electric bulb. He hurried down three flights to the black silent yard and began hunting backward and forward, combing with his fingers the lank grass round the base of the clothes-pole. He found it in the midden on a decayed cabbage leaf. It was smooth and round, the size of a glass marble, and it shone with a light which made it seem to rest on a precious bit of green and yellow velvet. He picked it up. It was warm and filled his cupped palm with a ruby glow. He put it in his pocket and went back upstairs.

That night in bed he had a closer look. He slept with his brother who was not easily wakened. Wriggling carefully far down under the sheets, he opened his palm and gazed. The star shone white and blue, making the space around him like a cave in an iceberg. He brought it close to his eye. In its depth was the pattern of a snow-flake, the grandest thing he had ever seen. He looked through the flake's crystal lattice into an ocean of glittering blue-black waves under a sky full of huge galaxies. He heard a remote lulling sound like the sound in a sea-shell, and fell asleep with the star safely clenched in his hand.

He enjoyed it for nearly two weeks, gazing at it each night below the sheets, sometimes seeing the snow-flake, sometimes a flower, jewel, moon or landscape. At first he kept it hidden during the day but soon took to carrying it about with him; the smooth rounded gentle warmth in his pocket gave comfort when he felt insulted or neglected.

At school one afternoon he decided to take a quick look. He was at the back of the classroom in a desk by himself. The teacher was among the boys at the front row and all heads were bowed over books. Quickly he brought out the star and looked. It contained an aloof eye with a cool green pupil which dimmed and trembled as if seen through water.

'What have you there, Cameron?'

He shuddered and shut his hand.

'Marbles are for the playground, not the classroom. You'd better give it to me.'

'I cannae, sir.'

'I don't tolerate disobedience, Cameron. Give me that thing.'

The boy saw the teacher's face above him, the mouth opening and shutting under a clipped moustache. Suddenly he knew what to do and put the star in his mouth and swallowed. As the warmth sank toward his heart he felt relaxed and at ease. The teacher's face moved into the distance. Teacher, classroom, world receded like a rocket into a warm, easy blackness leaving behind a trail of glorious stars, and he was one of them.

The star

C Did you enjoy the story? Give it a score for enjoyment: from 1 (not very enjoyable) to 5 (very enjoyable).

Find other students with the same score. Discuss your impressions of the story. Find students with scores very different from yours. Can you think of any reasons why your reactions should have been so different?

D In groups of three, re-tell the story in spoken English, in ten sentences, each person giving one sentence in turn.

E Here are the answers which one student gave when asked to say whether the following sentences are True (T) or False (F). DK means 'I don't know'. In pairs, decide which answers you would change.

Cameron had a deprived childhood.	F
Cameron didn't feel close to his brother.	DK
Cameron's parents were insensitive.	DK
The star was full of warmth and beauty.	F
The star made Cameron feel uneasy.	T
The teacher was firm but fair.	T
Cameron lost consciousness.	F

Read the story again.

F Concentrate on Cameron. What sort of boy does he seem to be? Study the extracts below and decide what they suggest about Cameron's personality. A few possibilities have been written in. You can add to these or change them before you go on to the others.

Extract from 'The star'	Quality suggested
A star had fallen beyond the horizon, in Canada perhaps. (He had an aunt in Canada.)	a daydreamer
Turning from the window he saw that no-one else had noticed.	
He said in a small voice, 'A'm gawn out.'	timid
He slipped through the lobby and onto the stairhead, banging the door after him.	resentful
He slept with his brother who was not easily wakened. Wriggling carefully far down under the sheets, he opened his palm and gazed.	
He heard a remote lulling sound like the sound in a sea-shell, and fell asleep with the star safely clenched in his hand.	

He enjoyed it for nearly two weeks, gazing at it each night below the sheets.	
At first he kept it hidden during the day but soon took to carrying it about with him; the smooth rounded gentle warmth in his pocket gave comfort when he felt insulted or neglected.	
At school one afternoon he decided to take a quick look. He was at the back of the classroom in a desk by himself.	
'What have you there, Cameron?' He shuddered and shut his hand.	
'You'd better give it to me.' 'I cannae, sir.'	*obstinate*
Suddenly he knew what to do and put the star in his mouth and swallowed. As the warmth sank toward his heart he felt relaxed and at ease.	

G Cameron lives in a tenement in Scotland. The discovery of the star offers a marvellous new world. Find expressions in the story which bring out this contrast and write them down under the headings below. The activity has been started for you.

Words/expressions which indicate poverty	Words/expressions which indicate the rich new world of the star
beyond the iron works	*a precious bit of green and yellow velvet*

When you have completed your columns, compare them with someone else's. Together try to decide what the marvellous world of the star could be. Could it be a dream of escape? Freedom? Friendship? Love?

The star

Creative development

Here are some further activities for you to choose from.

Mime

Prepare a mime to be performed while the story is being read aloud. If you can, select some suitable background music as further accompaniment to your mime.

Writing a different version

Imagine you are another child in Cameron's class. Write your version of the strange events that happened in the class that day.

Rewriting the story

(The class is divided into two halves.) One half: rewrite the story for a kindergarten class. The other half: rewrite it for a class of adult learners of English at elementary level.

Role-play

Work in groups of three. First prepare, then act out the dialogue that takes place between the schoolmaster and Cameron's parents after the story has ended.

Strange animal

an African story re-told by Alexander McCall Smith

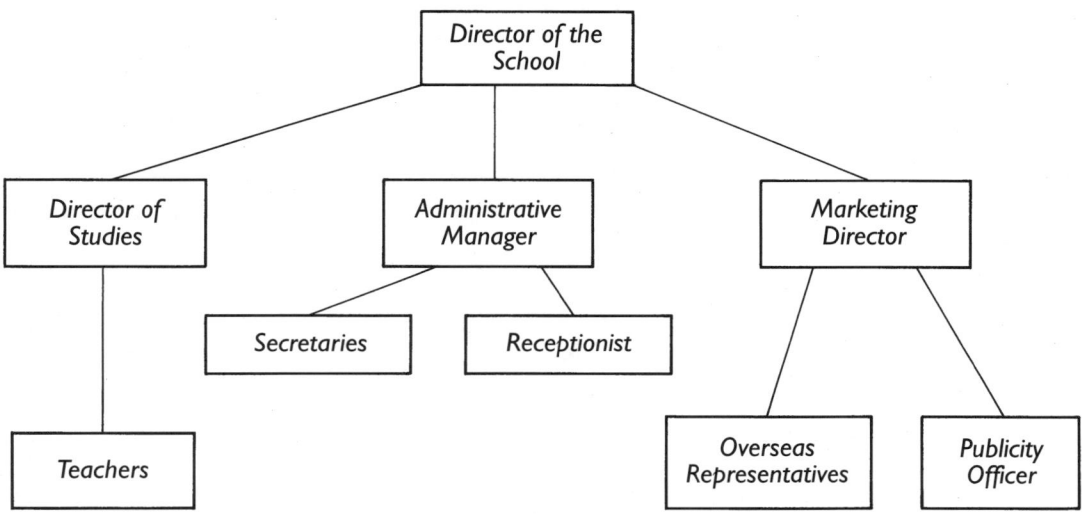

A This is the diagram of the organisation of a language school. It shows the lines of responsibility in the school. With a partner, look at the diagram and talk about it. Who tells who what to do in the school? Does the diagram tell you who makes the important decisions?

If you work for a company or another sort of organisation, would its diagram be very different? If you are in a school, is it organised like this?

B Now think of a family that has the following members.

child	younger sister
mother (the child's mother)	father (the child's father)
grandmother	uncle
grandfather	aunt
older brother	older sister

Draw a diagram like the one above to show your opinion: which people in the family should tell other people what to do? You can add other members of the family if you like.

Compare your diagram with those of others in your class. Discuss any differences.

Strange animal

C Look at the first paragraph of the story. With a partner, talk about the boy. What do you think his feelings are about his situation?

Read the first part of the story and listen to it on the cassette.

Part one

There were many people to tell that boy what to do. There was his mother and his father, his grandfather, and his older brother. And there was also an aunt, who was always saying: 'Do this. Do that.' Every day this aunt would shout at him, and make a great noise that would frighten the birds.

The boy did not like his aunt. Sometimes he thought that he might go to some man to buy some medicine to put into her food to make her quiet, but of course he never did this. In spite of all his aunt's shouting and ordering about, the boy always obeyed her, as his father said he must.

'She has nothing to do but shout at you,' the boy's father explained. 'It keeps her happy.'

'When I'm a big man I'll come and shout in her ear,' the boy said. It was good to think about that.

There was a place that the aunt knew where a lot of fruit grew. It was a place which was quite far away, and the boy did not like going there. Near this place there were caves and the boy had heard that a strange animal lived in these caves. One of his friends had seen this strange animal and had warned people about going near that place.

But the aunt insisted on sending the boy to pick fruit there, and so he went, his heart a cold stone of fear inside him. He found the trees and began to pick the fruit, but a little later he heard the sound of something in the bush beside him. He stopped his task and stood near the tree in case the strange animal should be coming.

Out of the bush came the strange animal. It was just as his friend had described it and the boy was very frightened. Quickly he took out the drum which he had brought with him and began to beat it. The strange animal stopped, looked at the boy in surprise, and began to dance.

All day the boy played the drum, keeping the strange animal dancing. As long as he played the drum, he knew that there was nothing that the strange animal could do to harm him. At last, when night came, the strange animal stopped dancing and disappeared back into the bush. The boy knew that it had gone back to its cave and so he was able to walk home safely. When he reached home, though, his aunt had prepared her shouting.

Strange animal

'Where is all the fruit?' she shouted. Thinking that he had eaten it, she then began to beat him until the boy was able to run away from her and hide in his own hut.

The boy told his father the next day of the real reason why he had been unable to bring back fruit from the tree. He explained that there had been a strange animal there and that he had had to play his drum to keep the animal dancing. The father listened and told the story to the aunt, who scoffed at the boy.

'There are no strange animals at that place,' she said. 'You must be making all this up.'

But the father believed the boy and said that the next day they would all go to the fruit place with him. The aunt thought that this was a waste of time, but she was not going to miss any chance of shouting, and so she came too.

When the family reached the tree there was no strange animal. The aunt began to pick fruit from the tree and stuff it into her mouth. Calling to the boy to give her his drum, she hung it on the branch of a tree in a place where he would not be able to get at it easily.

'You must pick fruit,' she shouted to the boy. 'You must not play a drum in idleness.'

The boy obeyed his aunt, but all the time he was listening for any sounds to come from the bush. He knew that sooner or later the strange animal would appear and that they would then all be in danger.

Strange animal

D With your partner, talk about this first part of the story. Make notes about the boy, the aunt and the father. You can use some of the words in the drum if they seem appropriate.

The boy	
The aunt	loud spiteful placatory quiet clever animal-loving timid sceptical firm diplomatic rebellious nasty headstrong peaceful sarcastic obedient brave noisy authoritarian reasonable strident kindly bossy well-meaning violent resourceful
The father	

E Decide what happens next – plan or write the end of the story. Change partners and discuss your endings.

Read the second part of the story and listen to it on the cassette.

Part two

When the strange animal did come, it went straight to the boy's father and mother and quickly ate them up. Then the aunt tried to run away, but the strange animal ran after her and ate her too. While this was happening, the boy had the time to reach up for his drum from the branch of the fruit tree. Quickly he began to play this drum, which made the strange animal stop looking for people to eat and begin to dance.

Strange animal

As the boy played his drum faster and faster, the strange animal danced more and more quickly. Eventually the boy played so fast that the animal had to spit out the father and the mother. The boy was very pleased with this and began to play more slowly. At this, the strange animal's dancing became slower.

'You must play your drum fast again,' the boy's father said. 'Then the strange animal will have to spit out your aunt.'

'Do I have to?' the boy asked, disappointed that he would not be allowed to leave the aunt in the stomach of the strange animal.

'Yes,' the boy's father said sternly. 'You must.'

Reluctantly, the boy again began to play the drum and the strange animal began to dance more quickly. After a few minutes it was dancing so quickly that it had to spit out the aunt. Then darkness came and the strange animal went back to its cave.

The aunt was very quiet during the journey back home. The next day she was quiet as well, and she never shouted at the boy again. Being swallowed by a strange animal had taught the aunt not to waste her time shouting; now, all that she wanted to do was to sit quietly in the sun.

The boy was very happy.

F Compare your reactions to the story. In groups, talk about any differences between your endings and the story's ending.

G Can you add anything to your notes about the boy, the aunt and the father? Which person changes the most because of what happens in the story?

H Folk tales often tell us something about the values of the society they come from. What values do you discern from your reading of this story? Choose two or three from this list or write your own.

Social harmony in the family is of paramount importance.
Pride comes before a fall.
Being eccentric or disruptive is not valued in the community.
Members of society must work together to ensure survival.
It is important to respect elders.
Tolerance is essential in the family and in the community.
People must live in harmony with their environment.
Others: ....
....

Creative development

Here are some further activities for you to choose from.

Representing the strange animal
Describe the 'strange animal'. If you were going to draw the strange animal for a book of folk tales for children, how would you represent it?

Creating a poster
Create a poster to be put near the fruit trees, warning people about the strange animal and telling them what to do if they see it.

Discussing folk tales
Sit in small groups and compare memories of folk tales you were told as a child. Are there any folk tales in your culture in which either a musical instrument has magical properties or someone is eaten (but doesn't necessarily die)?

Dramatising the story for children
Dramatise 'Strange animal' for a group of children at nursery school. You can choose one of these forms or one of your own.

- a mime with a simple version of the story told at the same time
- a mime with questions at key points to encourage children to guess what is happening
- shadow puppets
- a short one-act play

Writing a diary entry
Imagine that you are the aunt, coming home after the day of the events told in the story. Write an account of the day in your diary.

Hannah

by Malachi Whitaker

A Listen to the cassette and try to remember a party you went to when you were younger. When you are ready, compare your memories with those of someone else in the class.

Read the first part of the story and listen to it on the cassette.

Part one

The girl Hannah was seventeen, and she had made almost all that array of cakes and pastries on the kitchen dresser. She stood looking at them, her healthy pink face glowing with pride. She wore a blue dress and a white apron, and her hair waved down her back to her waist in a golden-brown shower.

The party should be a lovely one. All the girls from her Sunday-school class were coming, and four of the best-behaved boys as well. Then there was to be the young man, Thomas Henry Smithson, the one that all the girls secretly laughed at. Really, he was too conscientious, too lumberingly polite for anything. His hats seemed always small, his trousers tight, his boots big. But her mother liked him. He helped to make things go, sang a few songs in a voice he called baritone, and never lost his temper.

Hannah felt that she could put up with anything so long as Ralph Wellings turned up. He was nineteen. A strange boy for the little, fat, jolly parson to have as his son! Hannah had heard that he was wild, but he had never seemed wild to her. Sometimes they had met in the twilight, and he had walked along by her side through Pennyfoot woods to Hoyle's farm and carried the dozen eggs that she had gone to fetch back with him in a sugar-bag.

Of course, you were supposed to be still a child at seventeen, but Hannah didn't feel exactly like a child. She could talk to Ralph Wellings about the things she knew – the proper way to make candied toffee, the books she had recently found in the attic, old books in which all the letter esses were effs, the nicest hymn tunes. He never laughed at her, and she found this refreshing.

Hannah

She loved him very much, admiring his forehead, for some reason, most of all. It was high and white. His blue-black hair, parted at the side, waved as beautifully as did hers. 'If we get married and have some children, they're sure to have curly hair,' she thought. She liked, too, his flecked hazel eyes and his long fingers with their triangular nails. He called her 'nice child', and always seemed glad to see her.

She took her entranced gaze from the cakes and went into the dairy. The house had once been a farm, and the cool, stone-shelved room was still called the dairy. One side of it was laden with food. There was a whole, crumb-browned ham on a dish by the side of a meat-plate on which stood a perfectly cooked sirloin of beef. Another dish held four or five pounds of plump, cooked sausages. The trifles were ready, so were the stewed fruits for those who liked plainer sweets, and there was more cream, Hannah felt, than could possibly be used.

She ran out of the room, smiling with delight, to look for her mother.

'Are you getting ready, mother?' she called.

'Yes.'

Her mother stood, bare-armed, in front of the oval mirror, a worried look in her eyes, her mouth filled with steel hairpins. She had her skirt on, but her black satin bodice was flung over the curved bedrail.

'Aren't you washed, child?' She seemed to speak harshly because of the hairpins. 'The company'll be here before we know where we are. We sh'll have a rush, you'll see.'

'Never mind, mother, everything looks lovely. I wish the party was beginning just now.'

She ran out of the room and changed her dress in a perfect fury of speed. Her face was clean enough, her hands white. What was the use of washing over and over and over again? Now she was in the summer pink dress that made her look older than ever before. The skirt was flounced, and she jumped round ballooning it, running a comb through her hair at the same time.

'He'll like me, he'll like me, he will,' she chanted. And she ran across to her mother's room and flung herself panting on the great bed.

'Hannah, Hannah, be a lady!' cried her mother, rebukingly.

B With a partner, fill in as many of the squares below as you can.

	Appearance	Personality	Interests
Hannah			
Thomas Henry Smithson			
Ralph Wellings			

Compare your results.

C Think again about the party you remembered. What details of your party are like those described in the first part of the story: clothes? Food and drink? Guests? Hannah's feelings of anticipation?

D There are 23 lines left in this story. What do you think happens in those 23 lines? In pairs, make up a short ending. When you are ready, tell your ending to another group and listen to theirs.

Read the first part of the story again and then read the second part and listen to it on the cassette.

Part two

Hannah seemed to have been asleep for a long time. She woke slowly, feeling the grey light on her eyelids. Her hands, gnarled and shrunken, lay outside the blue-and-white coverlet. A shadowed white plait straggled over one shoulder, thinning to a thread-tied end as it reached her breast.

She moved a little, opened her eyes, and moistened her lips. The morning was sunny and still. It felt warm, warm. She dozed a little and went on thinking of the party her mother had given when she was seventeen. On that day Ralph Wellings had kissed her for the first time. Unknowingly she smiled. The pink dress with its flounces, she remembered that, too. How lovely it had all been.

She looked up when the door opened and frowned a little, seeing an ugly, middle-aged woman with a paper-backed book in her hand.

Hannah

'Well, grandma,' the woman said in a kind and cheerful voice, 'I've been up a few times, but you were asleep. George is just going to the Post Office in the doctor's car, so will you sign the pension form? He's in a bit of a hurry. I'll help you up.'

She put a soft wrap about the old woman's shoulders and supported her while she wrote. 'H-a-n-n-a-h' she mouthed, then her attention was attracted by something else for a moment. She stared at the completed form and gave a fretful cry. 'Oh, grandma, you've gone and done it again! We sh'll have no end of bother. You've signed Hannah Wellings, and your name's Smithson – Smithson – Smithson.'

E What do you think of this ending? In what ways is it different from the one you created?

What could possibly have happened between the first and second parts of the story? In small groups, think of as many possible explanations as you can, then choose the one you like best.

Creative development

Here are some further activities for you to choose from.

Discussing codes of behaviour

Hannah's mother tells her to 'be a lady'. Why? When Hannah was a young girl at the turn of the century, there was a difference between being a girl, and growing up to become 'a lady'. What about your country today? Are there kinds of behaviour that are acceptable, and others that are not, for a young girl nowadays? Write them down under the two columns.

A young girl can	A young girl cannot

Completing a script for a filmed version

Imagine that 'Hannah' is going to be made into a film. The director asks you to write a summary of the missing parts of Hannah's life, so that the film script can be complete.

The director would also like to give the film a new name, which will tell people more about the story. Choose an appropriate title.

An original piece of music is to be composed for the final section of the film, when Hannah, now an old lady, is dreaming of her youth. Which musical instrument or instruments do you think would be most appropriate? You can choose from this selection or suggest your own.

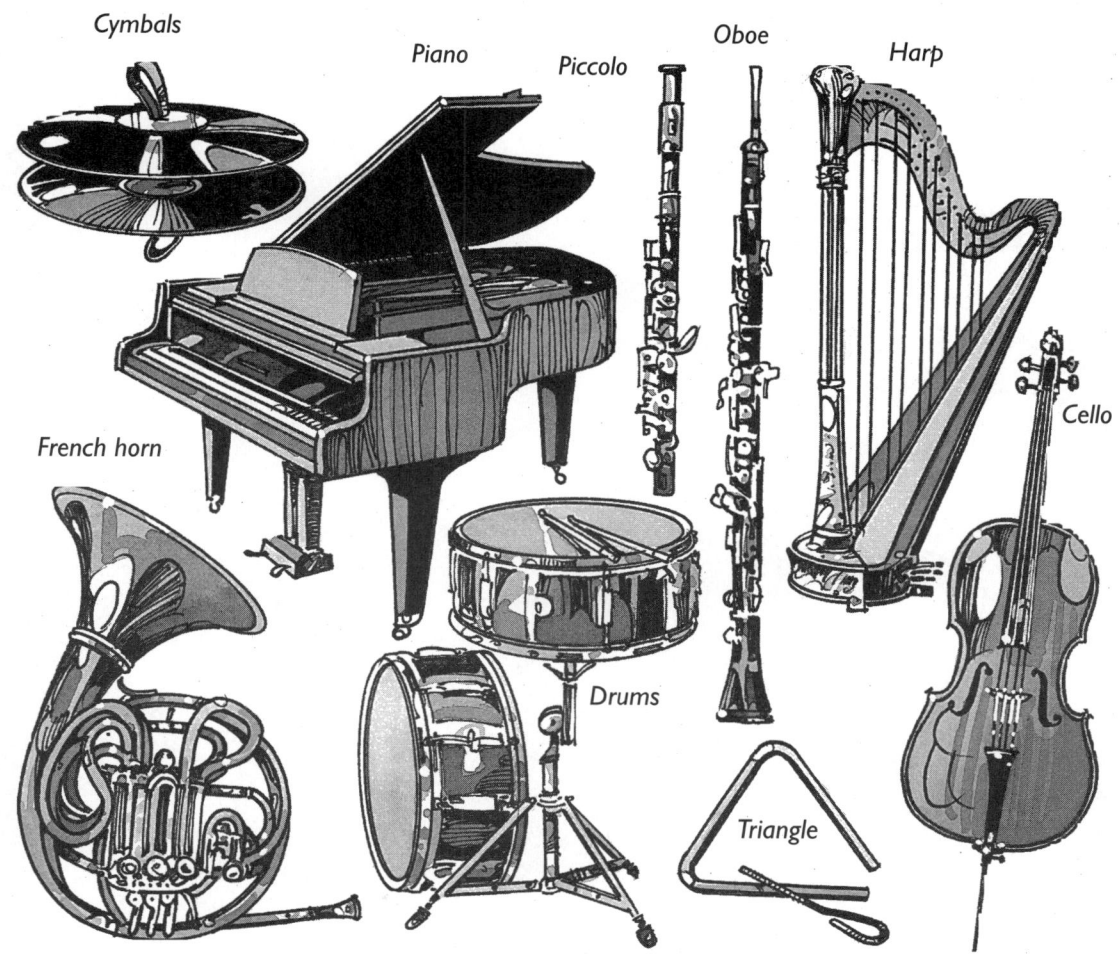

Hannah

Writing a diary entry

Write Hannah's diary entry for the night after the party.

Writing a poem

Imagine that you are Hannah. Write a poem entitled 'Regrets' by completing the following lines. You will see that the first letter of each line spells HANNAH whether you read the letters downwards … or upwards. If you prefer, you can write the poem about your own regrets, using your own name in the same way.

*H*ow I wish ....

A ....

N ....

N ....

A ....

*H*ow I wish ....

Report on the shadow industry

by Peter Carey

A Look at the words in the shape. Choose the three which, for you, best capture the meaning of the word 'shadow'. If you don't think the words are suitable, add some of your own.

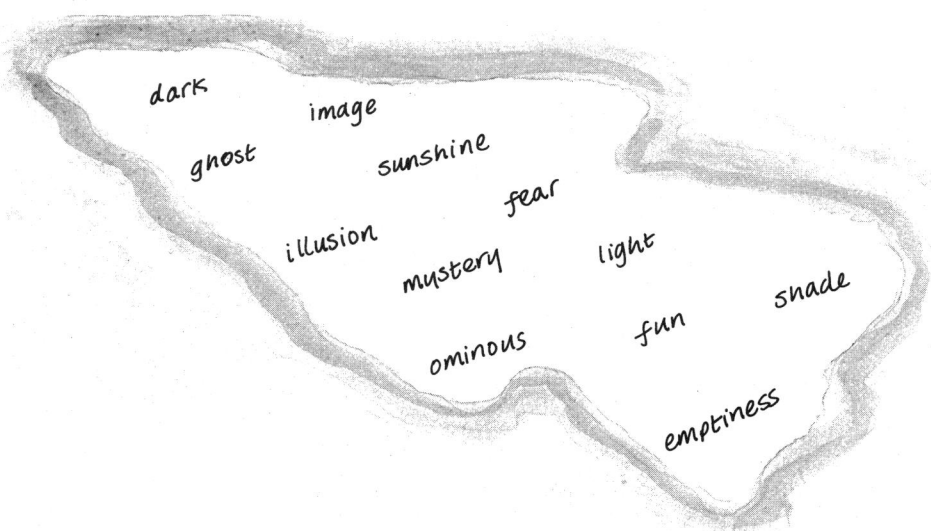

Compare your choices with other students'. Give reasons for your choices. Can you now agree on some essential features of a shadow, perhaps using some of the words you chose?

B The title contains the expression 'shadow industry'. What could that be? Discuss possible explanations.

Read the first part of the story and listen to it on the cassette.

Report on the shadow industry

1.

My friend S. went to live in America ten years ago and I still have the letter he wrote me when he first arrived, wherein he describes the shadow factories that were springing up on the west coast and the effects they were having on that society. 'You see people in dark glasses wandering around the supermarkets at 2 am. There are great boxes all along the aisles, some as expensive as fifty dollars but most of them only five. There's always Muzak. It gives me the shits more than the shadows. The people don't look at one another. They come to browse through the boxes of shadows although the packets give no indication of what's inside. It really depresses me to think of people going out at two in the morning because they need to try their luck with a shadow. Last week I was in a supermarket near Topanga and I saw an old negro tear the end off a shadow box. He was arrested almost immediately.'

A strange letter ten years ago but it accurately describes scenes that have since become common in this country. Yesterday I drove in from the airport past shadow factory after shadow factory, large faceless buildings gleaming in the sun, their secrets guarded by ex-policemen with alsatian dogs.

The shadow factories have huge chimneys that reach far into the sky, chimneys which billow forth smoke of different, brilliant colours. It is said by some of my more cynical friends that the smoke has nothing to do with any manufacturing process and is merely a trick, fake evidence that technological miracles are being performed within the factories. The popular belief is that the smoke sometimes contains the most powerful shadows of all, those that are too large and powerful to be packaged. It is a common sight to see old women standing for hours outside the factories, staring into the smoke.

There are a few who say the smoke is dangerous because of carcinogenic chemicals used in the manufacture of shadows. Others argue that the shadow is a natural product and by its very nature chemically pure. They point to the advantages of the smoke: the beautifully coloured patterns in the clouds which serve as a reminder of the happiness to be obtained from a fully realized shadow. There may be some merit in this last argument, for on cloudy days the skies above our city are a wondrous sight, full of blues and vermilions and brilliant greens which pick out strange patterns and shapes in the clouds.

Others say that the clouds now contain the dreadful beauty of the apocalypse.

Report on the shadow industry

C Do you consider these statements to be True (T) or False (F)? DK means 'I don't know'.

	T	F	DK
1 The shadow industry probably started in America.	☐	☐	☐
2 Boxes of shadows can be bought in supermarkets.	☐	☐	☐
3 Shadows are made in factories that give off thick, black smoke.	☐	☐	☐
4 Shadow factories have not spread to other countries.	☐	☐	☐
5 Some people think that the smoke from the factories is only for display.	☐	☐	☐
6 Some people think the factory smoke contains very powerful shadows.	☐	☐	☐
7 It is lawful to open shadow boxes and let the shadows escape.	☐	☐	☐
8 The shadows have a strong effect on people.	☐	☐	☐
9 People only buy them during the daytime.	☐	☐	☐
10 People examine the shadows before they buy them.	☐	☐	☐
11 Some people think the smoke contains chemicals that cause cancer.	☐	☐	☐
12 Some people believe that shadows bring happiness.	☐	☐	☐

Read the second part of the story and listen to it on the cassette.

2.

The shadows are packaged in large, lavish boxes which are printed with abstract designs in many colours. The Bureau of Statistics reveals that the average householder spends 25 per cent of his income on these expensive goods and that this percentage increases as the income decreases.

Report on the shadow industry

There are those who say that the shadows are bad for people, promising an impossible happiness that can never be realized and thus detracting from the very real beauties of nature and life. But there are others who argue that the shadows have always been with us in one form or another and that the packaged shadow is necessary for mental health in an advanced technological society. There is, however, research to indicate that the high suicide rate in advanced countries is connected with the popularity of shadows and that there is a direct statistical correlation between shadow sales and suicide rates. This has been explained by those who hold that the shadows are merely mirrors to the soul and that the man who stares into a shadow box sees only himself, and what beauty he finds there is his own beauty and what despair he experiences is born of the poverty of his spirit.

D What contradictory information is there about the shadows? Write notes under these two headings.

Arguments for shadows	Arguments against shadows

What new feelings do you now have about shadows?

Read the third and fourth parts of the story and listen to them on the cassette.

3.

I visited my mother at Christmas. She lives alone with her dogs in a poor part of town. Knowing her weakness for shadows I brought her several of the more expensive varieties which she retired to examine in the privacy of the shadow room.

She stayed in the room for such a long time that I became worried and knocked on the door. She came out almost immediately. When I saw her face I knew the shadows had not been good ones.

'I'm sorry,' I said, but she kissed me quickly and began to tell me about a neighbour who had won the lottery.

I myself know, only too well, the disappointments of shadow boxes for I also have a weakness in that direction. For me it is something of a guilty secret, something that would not be approved of by my clever friends.

I saw J. in the street. She teaches at the university.

'Ah-hah,' she said knowingly, tapping the bulky parcel I had hidden under my coat. I know she will make capital of this discovery, a little piece of gossip to use at the dinner parties she is so fond of. Yet I suspect that she too has a weakness for shadows. She confessed as much to me some years ago during that strange misunderstanding she still likes to call 'Our Affair'. It was she who hinted at the feeling of emptiness, that awful despair that comes when one has failed to grasp the shadow.

4.

My own father left home because of something he had seen in a box of shadows. It wasn't an expensive box, either, quite the opposite – a little surprise my mother had bought with the money left over from her housekeeping. He opened it after dinner one Friday night and he was gone before I came down to breakfast on the Saturday. He left a note which my mother only showed me very recently. My father was not good with words and had trouble communicating what he had seen: 'Words Cannot Express It What I Feel Because of The Things I Saw In The Box Of Shadows You Bought Me.'

Report on the shadow industry

E Make notes about shadows and the shadow industry. Decide whether your notes represent good things, bad things or neither good nor bad. The activity has been started for you.

Good things about shadows	Bad things about shadows	Neither good nor bad
you can get cheap ones		they're unpredictable

Work with a partner. Using your notes, summarise the effects of shadows on the narrator and their family.

Report on the shadow industry

Read the fifth part of the story and listen to it on the cassette.

5.

My own feelings about the shadows are ambivalent, to say the least. For here I have manufactured one more: elusive, unsatisfactory, hinting at greater beauties and more profound mysteries that exist somewhere before the beginning and somewhere after the end.

F The narrator says their feelings about shadows are 'ambivalent', that is, contradictory. But the narrator also claims to have manufactured one more shadow. In what ways could this short story itself be like a shadow?

G Now that you have read the whole story, what are your impressions of it? Circle any of the reaction words below that are close to your first impressions. Add your own reaction word(s) if you prefer.

really weird ~~depressing~~ ~~a bit puzzling~~
absolutely brilliant ~~complex ideas~~ boring
~~frustrating~~ difficult language not bad

Find others in the class with similar impressions to your own. Discuss the reasons for your choices.

Report on the shadow industry

Read the story again.

1.

My friend S. went to live in America ten years ago and I still have the letter he wrote me when he first arrived, wherein he describes the shadow factories that were springing up on the west coast and the effects they were having on that society. 'You see people in dark glasses wandering around the supermarkets at 2 am. There are great boxes all along the aisles, some as expensive as fifty dollars but most of them only five. There's always Muzak. It gives me the shits more than the shadows. The people don't look at one another. They come to browse through the boxes of shadows although the packets give no indication of what's inside. It really depresses me to think of people going out at two in the morning because they need to try their luck with a shadow. Last week I was in a supermarket near Topanga and I saw an old negro tear the end off a shadow box. He was arrested almost immediately.'

A strange letter ten years ago but it accurately describes scenes that have since become common in this country. Yesterday I drove in from the airport past shadow factory after shadow factory, large faceless buildings gleaming in the sun, their secrets guarded by ex-policemen with alsatian dogs.

The shadow factories have huge chimneys that reach far into the sky, chimneys which billow forth smoke of different, brilliant colours. It is said by some of my more cynical friends that the smoke has nothing to do with any manufacturing process and is merely a trick, fake evidence that technological miracles are being performed within the factories. The popular belief is that the smoke sometimes contains the most powerful shadows of all, those that are too large and powerful to be packaged. It is a common sight to see old women standing for hours outside the factories, staring into the smoke.

There are a few who say the smoke is dangerous because of carcinogenic chemicals used in the manufacture of shadows. Others argue that the shadow is a natural product and by its very nature chemically pure. They point to the advantages of the smoke: the beautifully coloured patterns in the clouds which serve as a reminder of the happiness to be obtained from a fully realized shadow. There may be some merit in this last argument, for on cloudy days the skies above our city are a wondrous sight, full of blues and vermilions and brilliant greens which pick out strange patterns and shapes in the clouds.

Others say that the clouds now contain the dreadful beauty of the apocalypse.

2.

The shadows are packaged in large, lavish boxes which are printed with abstract designs in many colours. The Bureau of Statistics reveals that the average householder spends 25 per cent of his income on these expensive goods and that this percentage increases as the income decreases.

There are those who say that the shadows are bad for people, promising an impossible happiness that can never be realized and thus detracting from the very real beauties of nature and life. But there are others who argue that the shadows have always been with us in one form or another and that the packaged shadow is necessary for mental health in an advanced technological society. There is, however, research to indicate that the high suicide rate in advanced countries is connected with the popularity of shadows and that there is a direct statistical correlation between shadow sales and suicide rates. This has been explained by those who hold that the shadows are merely mirrors to the soul and that the man who stares into a shadow box sees only himself, and what beauty he finds there is his own beauty and what despair he experiences is born of the poverty of his spirit.

3.

I visited my mother at Christmas. She lives alone with her dogs in a poor part of town. Knowing her weakness for shadows I brought her several of the more expensive varieties which she retired to examine in the privacy of the shadow room.

She stayed in the room for such a long time that I became worried and knocked on the door. She came out almost immediately. When I saw her face I knew the shadows had not been good ones.

'I'm sorry,' I said, but she kissed me quickly and began to tell me about a neighbour who had won the lottery.

I myself know, only too well, the disappointments of shadow boxes for I also have a weakness in that direction. For me it is something of a guilty secret, something that would not be approved of by my clever friends.

I saw J. in the street. She teaches at the university.

'Ah-hah,' she said knowingly, tapping the bulky parcel I had hidden under my coat. I know she will make capital of this discovery, a little piece of gossip to use at the dinner parties she is so fond of. Yet I suspect that she too has a weakness for shadows. She confessed as much to me some years ago during that strange misunderstanding she still likes to call 'Our Affair'. It was she who hinted at the feeling of emptiness, that awful despair that comes when one has failed to grasp the shadow.

4.

My own father left home because of something he had seen in a box of shadows. It wasn't an expensive box, either, quite the opposite – a little surprise my mother had bought with the money left over from her housekeeping. He opened it after dinner one Friday night and he was gone before I came down to breakfast on the Saturday. He left a note which my mother only showed me very recently. My father was not good with words and had trouble communicating what he had seen: 'Words Cannot Express It What I Feel Because of The Things I Saw In The Box Of Shadows You Bought Me.'

5.

My own feelings about the shadows are ambivalent, to say the least. For here I have manufactured one more: elusive, unsatisfactory, hinting at greater beauties and more profound mysteries that exist somewhere before the beginning and somewhere after the end.

H What for you is the most powerful sentence in each of the five sections? In groups, compare your five choices and explain your reasons for them.

Creative development

Here are some further activities for you to choose from.

Mime
Imagine you have just opened a spectacular box of shadows and have become speechless as a result. Using mime only, no words, try to communicate to your friends the wonderful things you saw.

Writing instructions
Write a set of instructions to be pasted on the side of a box of shadows.

Painting a mind picture

Imagine you have been asked to paint a picture based on 'Report on the shadow industry'. What colours – and what images – seem to be appropriate? Discuss your selections. Use the colours named on the palette below. Close your eyes and listen to the story again on cassette if that will help you to imagine the colours and images.

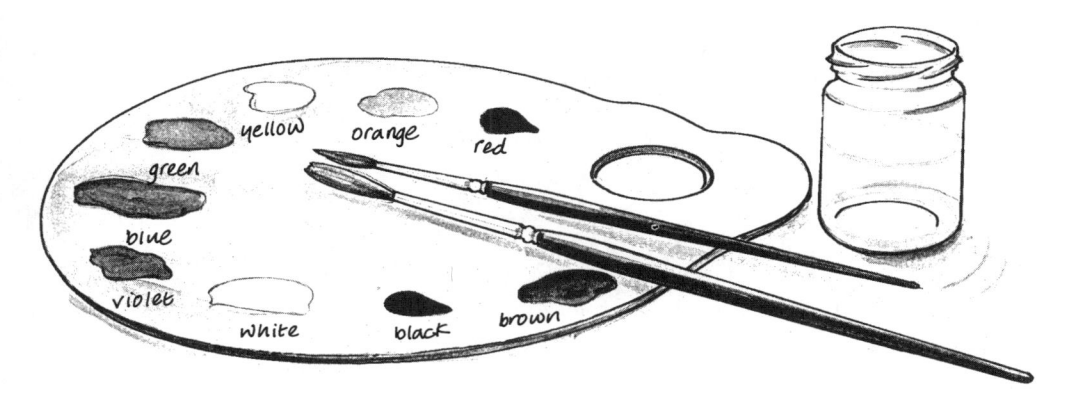

Reactions to the story

Read what one student wrote about 'Report on the shadow industry'. Do you agree with the assessment? Either write your comments on it or write your own final assessment of the story.

> This is a very complex story. The most approximate meaning of the shadows is that they are mirrors of our true selves. The reasons why people commit suicide after looking at their shadows could be either because they are scared of the ugliness of their spirit or because what they've seen is something so beautiful and enlightening that they no longer want to live on this planet, but want to live with the shadow.
>
> Everybody seems disappointed with their own shadows. I suppose nobody has reached total perfection and purity of spirit which in my opinion is unattainable, intangible, just like a shadow.

Report on the shadow industry

Asking questions and summarising

From the list below, choose two or three questions that you would like to have answered. Make up your own if you prefer.

Sit in small groups and ask your chosen questions. The other students will try to answer them. If you wish, ask your teacher the same questions. When you are satisfied, write a short summary of the points you found most interesting in the answers you were given.

1. Is the story set in the future or does it take place now? Give reasons.
2. Why do people buy shadow boxes, do you think?
3. What do you think 'apocalypse' means (Part 1, last word)?
4. Have you ever read a story which is in any way similar to this one? If so, can you re-tell it?
5. Would you like to read more stories by this writer? Give reasons for your answer.
6. On the whole, are the shadows harmful or beneficial? Why?
7. Which of the following words best captures the mood of the story and why?
   a) despair   b) mystery   c) emptiness   d) futility
   e) another (name it) ....
8. What is in the shadow boxes – or what do they represent?
9. Add your own: ....

Quickwriting about shadows

First, prepare a blank sheet of paper and a pen or pencil. Then, spend a few minutes thinking quietly about shadows. Try to gather in your mind all your impressions about shadows after reading this story.

Then start writing about shadows and keep on writing steadily for two minutes, or until your teacher tells you to stop. Do not take your pencil off the page and do not worry about grammar or English expression – just let your pen write down anything that is in your mind.

When you have finished, briefly tell another student the two or three main points of what you have written, and listen to their summary. Tell the other student what you liked best in their summary.

Verbal transcription — 6 a.m.

by William Carlos Williams

A Consider this situation.

Someone in your home has suddenly woken up early in the morning with a terrible pain. You call the doctor. When the doctor arrives an hour later, the situation is the same. You open the door to let the doctor in.

With another student, write the conversation that then takes place. Try to use one or more of the expressions in the diagram.

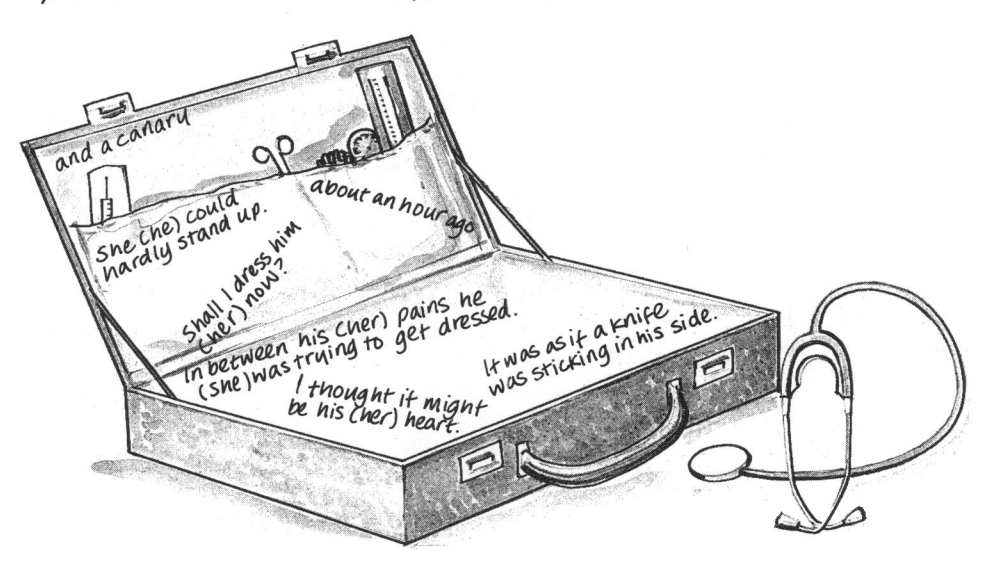

Expressions in the diagram:
- and a canary
- She (he) could hardly stand up.
- Shall I dress him (her) now?
- about an hour ago
- In between his (her) pains he (she) was trying to get dressed.
- It was as if a knife was sticking in his side.
- I thought it might be his (her) heart.

When you are ready, perform your conversation for another pair, and then listen to theirs. Compare these aspects of your conversations.

	Conversation 1	Conversation 2
The number of speakers, and who they are		
The speaker who says the most		

What other similarities and differences are there between your two scenes?

Verbal transcription – 6 a.m.

B Listen to 'Verbal transcription – 6 a.m.' It concerns a situation like the one you have just considered. As you listen, identify how many speakers there are. With a partner, jot down the details you can remember. Compare your notes and your impressions with those of others in the room.

Read the story and listen to it on the cassette.

THE WIFE:

About an hour ago. He woke up and it was as if a knife was sticking in his side. I tried the old reliable, I gave him a good drink of whisky but this time it did no good. I thought it might be his heart so I … Yes. In between his pains he was trying to get dressed. He could hardly stand up but through it all he was trying to get himself ready to go to work. Can you imagine that?

Rags! Leave the man alone. The minute you're good to him he … Look at him sitting up and begging! Rags! Come here! Do you want to look out of the window? Oh, yes. That's his favorite amusement – like the rest of the family. And we're not willing just to look out. We have to lean out as if we were living on Third Avenue.

Two dogs killed our old cat last week. He was thirteen years old. That's unusual for a cat, I think. We never let him come upstairs. You know he was stiff and funny looking. But we fed him and let him sleep in the cellar. He was deaf and I suppose he couldn't fight for himself and so they killed him.

Yes. We have quite a menagerie. Have you seen our blue-jay? He had a broken wing. We've had him two years now. He whistles and answers us when we call him. He doesn't look so good but he likes it here. We let him out of the cage sometimes with the window open. He goes to the sill and looks out. Then he turns and runs for his cage as if he was scared. Sometimes he sits on the little dog's head and they are great friends. If he went out I'm afraid he wouldn't understand and they would kill him too.

And a canary. Yes. You know I was afraid it was his heart. Shall I dress him now? This is the time he usually takes the train to be there at seven o'clock. Pajamas are so cold. Here put on this old shirt – this old horse blanket, I always call it. I'm sorry to be such a fool but those

Verbal transcription – 6 a.m.

needles give me a funny feeling all over. I can't watch you give them. Thank you so much for coming so quickly. I have a cup of coffee for you all ready in the kitchen.

C Here are some inferences about the story. Which do you agree with? Add some of your own if you wish.

    The woman in the story is elderly.
    She is more concerned with her pets than with the sick man.
    The sick man is her husband.
    She is lonely.
    She is kind-hearted.
    She is suffering from shock.
    She doesn't care too much about the sick man.
    The sick man is unconscious.
    She accepts the situation calmly.
    The woman's home is in the country not in the city.
    The woman is a bit odd.

    ....
    ....

Talk about your choices with others.

D Compare this story with the conversation that you wrote. Do you think that you know a lot about your characters, or do you think you know more about the characters in 'Verbal transcription – 6 a.m.'? Discuss this with one or two others.

Creative development

Here are some further activities for you to choose from.

Writing an interior monologue

The sick man in the story says absolutely nothing. Imagine he is having an 'interior monologue' – that is, he is talking to himself – at the same time as the wife is talking. With another student list some of his possible thoughts at this time. Then write them as an unbroken monologue.

Imagining the doctor's replies

The doctor is silent in the story, yet he seems to be asking questions and is clearly attending to his patient. In a group, decide on the sorts of questions, comments and replies the doctor is making. Write a list of the doctor's questions and any other comments he may be making during his visit. Make little marks in the text to show where the doctor speaks.

Verbal transcription – 6 a.m.

Discussing panic

Think again of the conversation you wrote at the beginning. If you really had to call a doctor for someone who was seriously ill, would you panic in any of these ways?

> rush around
> shout
> 'freeze' on the spot with shock
> become very clumsy – drop things, knock things over …
> lose your ability to concentrate

How do you manage your emotions in emergency situations? The wife in the story is definitely not panicking. Do you consider this somewhat strange, given the circumstances? Talk about this in groups. Would you be able to remain as cool as the woman in the story?

Discussing and illustrating a theme

One of the themes of the story is that ordinary life goes on even in the middle of emergency situations. In the wife's monologue, details of ordinary life intermingle with details about the man's condition. With another student, put these extracts under the appropriate heading. Add a few more details from the story.

> *I gave him a good drink of whisky*
> *Look at him sitting up and begging!*
> *Do you want to look out of the window?*
> *Have you seen our blue-jay?*
> *Shall I dress him now?*
> *Pajamas are so cold.*
> *I have a cup of coffee for you all ready in the kitchen.*

Emergency situation	Ordinary life

Verbal transcription – 6 a.m.

This theme of ordinary life and extraordinary events happening at the same time is often used to create a humorous effect. Look at this cartoon. How does it illustrate the theme?

"George has always liked foreign food."

This could be a cartoon representation of the story. In pairs, supply a caption.

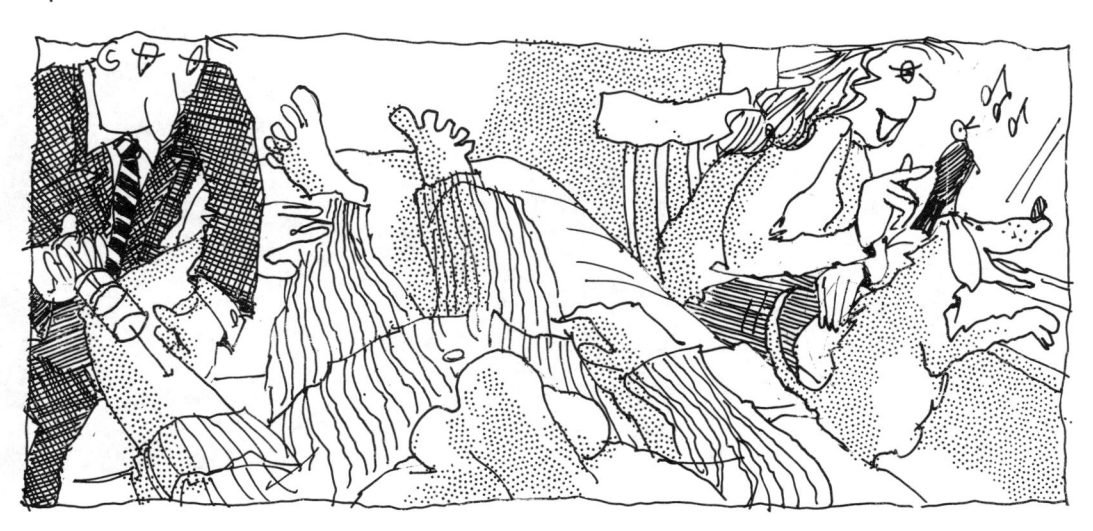

Read out your captions to the class.

The debutante

by Leonora Carrington

A With a few other students, look at this selection of pictures. Talk about your reactions to them. Can you see anything that they have in common? Exchange ideas.

The debutante

B Some artists who produced work like the pictures on the opposite page have tried to explain their aims. Here are some extracts from what they have written. Which ones seem to be relevant to the pictures you have been looking at? Talk about this with other students.

'… the resolution of … two states … dream and reality'

'… access to the depths of the self … , to the irrational, to the impulses that spring from the dark side of the soul'

'… insolence and playfulness …'

'… an obstinate dedication to fight everything repressive in conventional wisdom'

'And first of all we'll destroy this civilisation that is so dear to you … Western world, you are condemned to death.'

C Before you start reading, write some of your ideas in the empty squares. Work with another student.

	usually suggests
A debutante	a young woman a ball being presented at a royal court dancing wealth eligibility for marriage beautiful clothes and wonderful food expensive 'finishing' school (specialising in the social education of young ladies)
A hyena	

Compare your ideas with those produced by other pairs. What are the common features of your views of a hyena?

39

The debutante

Read the story for the first time and listen to it on the cassette.

When I was a debutante, I often went to the zoo. I went so often that I knew the animals better than I knew girls of my own age. Indeed it was in order to get away from people that I found myself at the zoo every day. The animal I got to know best was a young hyena. She knew me too. She was very intelligent. I taught her French, and she, in return, taught me her language. In this way we passed many pleasant hours.

My mother was arranging a ball in my honour on the first of May. During this time I was in a state of great distress for whole nights. I've always detested balls, especially when they are given in my honour.

On the morning of the first of May 1934, very early, I went to visit the hyena.

'What a bloody nuisance,' I said to her. 'I've got to go to my ball tonight.'

'You're very lucky,' she said. 'I'd love to go. I don't know how to dance, but at least I could make small talk.'

'There'll be a great many different things to eat,' I told her. 'I've seen truckloads of food delivered to our house.'

'And you're complaining,' replied the hyena, disgusted. 'Just think of me, I eat once a day, and you can't imagine what a heap of bloody rubbish I'm given.'

I had an audacious idea, and I almost laughed. 'All you have to do is to go instead of me!'

'We don't resemble each other enough, otherwise I'd gladly go,' said the hyena rather sadly.

'Listen,' I said. 'No one sees too well in the evening light. If you disguise yourself, nobody will notice you in the crowd. Besides, we're practically the same size. You're my only friend, I beg you to do this for me.'

She thought this over, and I knew that she really wanted to accept.

'Done,' she said all of a sudden.

There weren't many keepers about, it was so early in the morning. I opened the cage quickly, and in a very few moments we were out in the street. I hailed a taxi; at home, everybody was still in bed. In my room I brought out the dress I was to wear that evening. It was a little long, and the hyena found it difficult to walk in my high-heeled shoes. I found some gloves to hide her hands, which were too hairy to look like mine. By the time the sun was shining into my room, she was able to make her way around the room several times, walking more or less upright. We were so busy that my mother almost opened the door to say good morning before the hyena had hidden under my bed.

'There's a bad smell in your room,' my mother said, opening the window. 'You must have a scented bath before tonight, with my new bath salts.'

'Certainly,' I said.

She didn't stay long. I think the smell was too much for her.

'Don't be late for breakfast,' she said and left the room.

The greatest difficulty was to find a way of disguising the hyena's face. We spent hours and hours looking for a way, but she always rejected my suggestions. At last she said, 'I think I've found the answer. Have you got a maid?'

'Yes,' I said, puzzled.

'There you are then. Ring for your maid, and when she comes in we'll pounce upon her and tear off her face. I'll wear her face tonight instead of mine.'

'It's not practical,' I said. 'She'll probably die if she hasn't got a face. Somebody will certainly find the corpse, and we'll be put in prison.'

'I'm hungry enough to eat her,' the hyena replied.

'And the bones?'

'As well,' she said. 'So, it's on?'

'Only if you promise to kill her before tearing off her face. It'll hurt her too much otherwise.'

'All right. It's all the same to me.'

Not without a certain amount of nervousness I rang for Mary, my maid. I certainly wouldn't have done it if I didn't hate having to go to a ball so much. When Mary came in I turned to the wall so as not to see. I must admit it didn't take long. A brief cry, and it was over. While the hyena was eating, I looked out the window. A few minutes later she said, 'I can't eat any more. Her two feet are left over still, but if you have a little bag, I'll eat them later in the day.'

'You'll find a bag embroidered with fleurs-de-lis in the cupboard. Empty out the handkerchiefs you'll find inside, and take it.' She did as I suggested. Then she said, 'Turn round now and look how beautiful I am.'

In front of the mirror, the hyena was admiring herself in Mary's face. She had nibbled very neatly all around the face so that what was left was exactly what was needed.

'You've certainly done that very well,' I said.

Towards evening, when the hyena was all dressed up, she declared, 'I really feel in tip-top form. I have a feeling that I shall be a great success this evening.'

The debutante

When we had heard the music from downstairs for quite some time, I said to her, 'Go on down now, and remember, don't stand next to my mother. She's bound to realise that it isn't me. Apart from her I don't know anybody. Best of luck.' I kissed her as I left her, but she did smell very strong.

Night fell. Tired by the day's emotions, I took a book and sat down by the open window, giving myself up to peace and quiet. I remember that I was reading *Gulliver's Travels* by Jonathan Swift. About an hour later, I noticed the first signs of trouble. A bat flew in at the window, uttering little cries. I am terribly afraid of bats. I hid behind a chair, my teeth chattering. I had hardly gone down on my knees when the sound of beating wings was overcome by a great noise at my door. My mother entered, pale with rage.

'We'd just sat down at table,' she said, 'when that thing sitting in your place got up and shouted, 'So I smell a bit strong, what? Well, I don't eat cakes!' Whereupon it tore off its face and ate it. And with one great bound, disappeared through the window.'

D Write down three words or phrases which summarise your immediate reactions to the story.

....

....

....

Compare your reaction words, and try to explain your reasons for choosing them.

Read the story again.

E As you read, jot down words or phrases in this grid.

	The debutante	The hyena	The mother
Appearance			
Behaviour			

Work with a partner. Using your completed grid, describe each one of the main characters in the story. Add your own opinions. What do you think of each? What are they like as individuals?

Some dictionaries describe hyenas as 'cruel', 'treacherous', 'rapacious'. In the story, who is more cruel, in your view – the debutante or the hyena?

F Look again at the pictures and the ideas that you considered before reading the story. Which of the following aspects do you think is dominant in this particular story? Add others if you wish.

> the overlap between dream and reality
> an attack on the social behaviour of the bourgeoisie in Western civilisation
> the deep impulses and irrational elements within us all
> ....
> ....

Talk about your thoughts together.

Creative development

Here are some further activities for you to choose from.

Discussing reactions to the story
Who could you give this story to?

> some of your friends
> elderly relatives
> work colleagues

What reaction would you anticipate getting from these people? Discuss this with other students.

Writing a conversation
Write the conversation that takes place the next day when the debutante visits her friend the hyena at the zoo.

The debutante

Discussing interpretations

Read this comment on 'The debutante'.

> The importance of the hyena is that it represents part of every human person – the animal lust (the hyena has a terrific appetite) and dark sensuality (it smells strongly) just hiding under a human face. So in reality the hyena and the debutante are two sides of the same person – human beings are nice and polite on the surface, but just wild beasts deep inside.

If we imagine the debutante in that way as half woman, half hyena, does that alter our view of the story? In a small group, discuss this interpretation.

In the mythology of many ancient civilisations there is a half human / half animal being, such as the minotaur, the centaur or the sphinx. It signifies a union of human and animal characteristics.

In small groups, think of some prominent personalities from your own society and make them into mythical half-beasts for posterity. For example: a graceful dancer might become half human / half swan or a ruthless politician might be half wolf / half human.

In your group, discuss the qualities of the new combination. Would a more honest, a more interesting – or a more vicious – creature be the result?

Adapting the story

In what ways does this story remind you of a horror film? Could it be successfully adapted as a short horror film, do you think? With another student, talk about how you, as a film maker, would depict the more gruesome parts of the tale (killing and eating the maid, fixing her face on to the hyena, tearing off the face and eating it …).

Would you
- suggest the horror rather than show it literally, and build up suspense in other ways?
- show the horror graphically and shock the unsuspecting audience?
- use some other device?

Writing a horror story

Do modern horror stories and films fascinate you or bore you? Talk about some you have seen or read and the impact they had.

Write the first paragraph of a horror story, beginning:

The branches of the apple tree scraped the window, casting craggy shadows on the moonlit wall by my bed. But there were other noises, strange, half-human moans …

The debutante

Guessing and finding out about the author

What sort of person might write a story of this kind? With another student, try to imagine the author. Write down your ideas or your guesses next to these questions.

Where was she born? ....
What kind of family did she come from? ....
What kind of education did she have? ....
What was she good at? ....
Was she married? ....
Was she conventional or rebellious? ....
Did she live most of her life in one place, or did she travel a lot?
....

Compare your guesses with those around you.

🎧 Listen to a short talk about Leonora Carrington's actual life. As you listen jot down notes about her next to these headings.

Birth: ....
Parents: ....
Education: ....
Ambition: ....
Relationships: ....
Marriages: ....
Children: ....
Places where she lived: ....
Talents: ....

Compare your guesses with the description you listened to. Are you surprised?

Here is a self-portrait painted by Leonora Carrington (in 1936–37). What similarities can you see between the painting and the story?

Important things

by Barbara L. Greenberg

A What should parents tell their children, and when? In groups think about a child's life from the age of five years up to 15 years old. Together, decide on a list of the most important things that parents should tell their children in those years. Consider these and add your own.

    death (of people and animals)
    facts of life
    religious beliefs
    facts about the planet and the universe
    rules of behaviour (don't lie; don't talk to strangers …)

    5–7   8–10   11–12   13–15

Read the story for the first time and listen to it on the cassette.

For years the children whimpered and tugged. 'Tell us, tell us.'

You promised to tell the children some other time, later, when they were old enough.

Now the children stand eye to eye with you and show you their teeth. 'Tell us.'

'Tell you what?' you ask, ingenuous.

'Tell us The Important Things.'

You tell your children there are six continents and five oceans, or vice versa.

You tell your children the little you know about sex. Your children tell you there are better words for what you choose to call The Married Embrace.

Important things

You tell your children to be true to themselves. They say they are true to themselves. You tell them they're lying, you always know when they're lying. They tell you you're crazy. You tell them to mind their manners. They think you mean it as a joke; they laugh.

There are tears in your eyes. You tell the children the dawn will follow the dark, the tide will come in, the grass will be renewed, every dog will have its day. You tell them the story of The Littlest Soldier whose right arm, which he sacrificed while fighting for a noble cause, grew back again.

You say that if there were no Evil we wouldn't have the satisfaction of choosing The Good. And if there were no pain, you say, we'd never know our greatest joy, relief from pain.

You offer to bake a cake for the children, a fudge cake with chocolate frosting, their favorite.

'Tell us,' say the children.

You say to your children, 'I am going to die.'

'When?'

'Someday.'

'Oh.'

You tell your children that they, too, are going to die. They already knew it.

You can't think of anything else to tell the children. You say you're sorry. You *are* sorry. But the children have had enough of your excuses.

'A promise is a promise,' say the children.

They'll give you one more chance to tell them of your own accord. If you don't, they'll have to resort to torture.

B We asked some people for their first impressions of this story. Here are some of the things they said. Look at the comments with another student. Are any of them similar to your own first impressions?

- It's very difficult because it says so much in such a short space.
- I think it's really beautiful – children are just like that; they never stop asking.
- It's so frustrating – makes you want to strangle those children.
- It's quite chilling really – when you think of things like 'they show you their teeth', what are they actually doing – snarling?
- It really builds up a picture of parents and children and how the relation changes as they get older.

Important things

📖 **Read the story again.**

C Here is a summary of the things that the parent says to the children at different times. The children's reaction is sometimes stated and sometimes we have to imagine it. With a partner, add your ideas about the children's reaction in the right-hand column.

Parent	Children
Promises to tell them when they are older.	whimper and tug
Tells them about the physical world.	
Tells them a bit about sex.	They already know more.
Gives advice about behaviour.	
Gives them conventional wisdom in the form of well-known sayings.	
Tells them a story with a moral.	
Tries to explain the existence of evil.	They continue to ask, so they are not impressed.
Offers them something nice to eat as a diversion.	
Tells them about the parent's death.	
Tells them about their own death.	

D If the children keep asking to be told the important things, and the parent can never find an answer that satisfies them, what point do you think the story is making? Do any of the following statements satisfy you? In a small group, discuss your ideas.

There are no answers to the important questions in life.
Differences between people will always separate them.
One generation will never be content with another generation's knowledge.
There are no important things in the end: you just go on living.

Important things

Creative development

Here are some further activities for you to choose from.

Discussing lessons learnt

Think about your own life. What did your parents try to impress upon you? What lessons have you learnt from your own experiences? Write a few notes under each heading and then exchange ideas with others in the class.

Things I've learnt by experience	Things my parents tried to teach me

Writing advice

Imagine you are giving advice to a younger person. Complete these sentences, so that you are giving your own opinions.

The important thing to remember about education is ....
....
....

One of the most important things about a job is ....
....
....

In relationships, what's important is ....
....
....

When you're going through a rough patch, it's important to ....
....
....

The important thing about ....
....
....

See what other people have written. Is there much variation in what people think?

Important things

Choosing/discussing the five most important things in life

In a survey in Europe some years ago, young people were asked what they thought the most important things in life were. Choose five of these and rank them. You can use some of your own if you prefer.

- good health
- pleasant surroundings
- a well-paid job
- time to yourself
- peace of mind
- honesty
- a clear conscience
- a happy, durable relationship
- an interesting job
- exciting holidays
- good food
- being able to help other people
- lots of money
- a happy family life
- good behaviour
- a satisfying job
- a nice house

Dialogue writing with proverbs

Look at these proverbs which have been split into halves. Try to put the halves together to form the original sayings.

Every dog will have	a silver lining.
Pride goes	is a virtue.
Every cloud has	is bliss.
A rolling stone	before a fall.
Least said	its day.
Look	repent at leisure.
Patience	gathers no moss.
Ignorance	before you leap.
Marry in haste	is worth two in the bush.
A bird in the hand	soonest mended.

In a small group, continue the story by writing a dialogue between the parent and the children. Use one proverb in the parent's speech and another in the children's. Act out your dialogue for another group.

Secrets

by Tim Winton

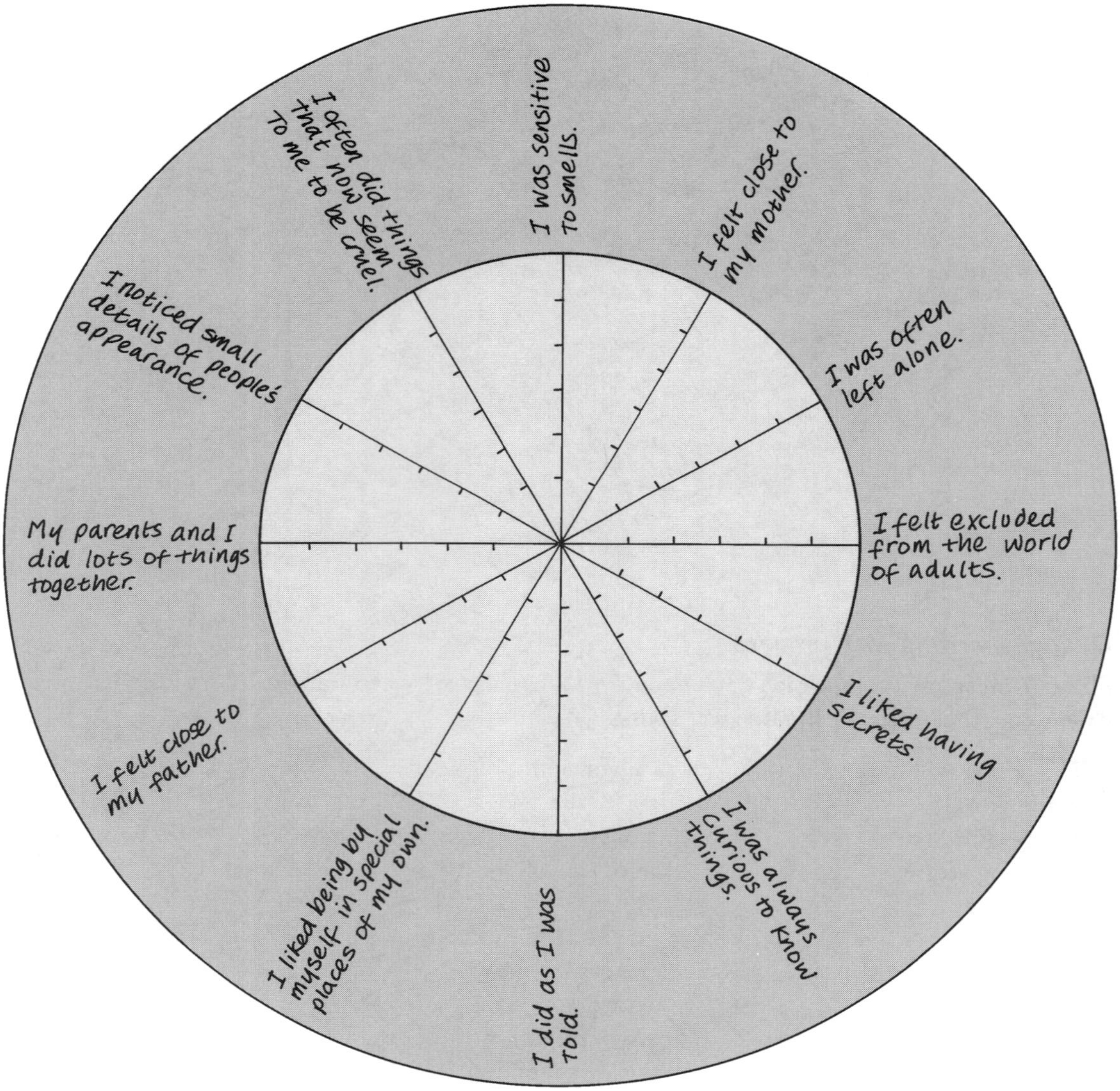
I was sensitive to smells.
I felt close to my mother.
I was often left alone.
I felt excluded from the world of adults.
I liked having secrets.
I was always curious to know things.
I did as I was told.
I liked being by myself in special places of my own.
I felt close to my father.
My parents and I did lots of things together.
I noticed small details of people's appearance.
I often did things that now seem to me to be cruel.

Secrets

A Put a cross on each line in the circle, at an appropriate point, to show how you felt as a child. The scale goes from

             0   →   6
      not at all   very much

Join the crosses with a pencil line.

Compare your pattern with your neighbour's, and talk about it. Is there anyone near to you with a similar pattern? Talk about similarities or differences in your childhood memories.

B Here is a summary of the beginning of 'Secrets', a story about a girl called Kylie. As you listen to the beginning of the story, fill in the missing details.

> Kylie lives in Australia. She and her mother have moved to a new house with ...., her mother's friend. Kylie misses her .... She's exploring the .... and finds an egg. Nobody else knows about the nice, ... egg. She feels happy because now she has a ....

Check your answers with other students. Imagine how the story might develop. Compare your ideas with others in the class.

Read the first part of the story and listen to it on the cassette.

Part one

Out the back of the new house, between the picket fence and a sheet of tin, Kylie found an egg. Her mother and Philip were inside. She heard them arguing and wished she still lived with her father. The yard was long and excitingly littered with fallen grapevines, a shed, lengths of timber and wire, and twitching shadows from big trees. It wasn't a new house, but it was new to her. She had been exploring the yard. The egg was white and warm-looking in its nest of dirt and down. Reaching in, she picked it up and found that it was warm. She looked back at the house. No one was watching. Something rose in her chest: now she knew what it was to have a secret.

   At dinner her mother and Philip spoke quietly to one another and drank from the bottle she was only allowed to look at. Her mother was a tall woman with short hair like a boy. One of her front teeth had gone brown and it made Kylie wonder. She knew that Philip was Mum's new husband, only they weren't married. He smelt of cigarettes and moustache hairs. Kylie thought his feet were the shape of pasties.

When everything on her plate was gone, Kylie left the table. Because the loungeroom was a jungle of boxes and crates inside one of which was the TV, she went straight to her new room. She thought about the egg as she lay in bed. She was thinking about it when she fell asleep.

Next day, Kylie got up onto the fence and crabbed all around it looking into the neighbours' yards. The people behind had a little tin shed and a wired-up run against the fence in which hens and a puff-chested little rooster pecked and picked and scruffled. So, she thought, balanced on the splintery grey fence, that's where the egg comes from. She climbed down and checked behind the sheet of tin and found the egg safe but cold.

Later, she climbed one of the big trees in the yard, right up, from where she could observe the hens and the rooster next door. They were fat, white birds with big red combs and bright eyes. They clucked and preened and ruffled and Kylie grew to like them. She was angry when the piebald rooster beat them down to the ground and jumped on their backs, pecking and twisting their necks. All his colours were angry colours; he looked mean.

Inside the house Mum and Philip laughed or shouted and reminded her that Dad didn't live with them any more. It was good to have a secret from them, good to be the owner of something precious. Philip laughed at the things she said. Her mother only listened to her with a smile that said *you don't know a single true thing*.

Sometime in the afternoon, after shopping with her mother, Kylie found a second egg in the place between the fence and the tin. She saw, too, a flash of white beneath a mound of vine cuttings in the corner of the yard. She climbed her tree and waited. A hen, thinner and more raggedy than the others, emerged. She had a bloody comb and a furtive way of pecking the ground alertly and moving in nervous bursts. For some time, she poked and scratched about, fossicking snails and slugs out of the long grass, until Kylie saw her move across to the piece of tin and disappear.

Each day Kylie saw another egg added to the nest up the back. She saw the raggedy hen pecked and chased and kicked by the others next door, saw her slip between the pickets to escape. The secret became bigger every day. The holidays stretched on. Philip and her mother left her alone. She was happy. She sat on the fence, sharing the secret with the hen.

When they had first moved into this house on the leafy, quiet street, Philip had shown Kylie and her mother the round, galvanized tin cover of the bore well in the back of the yard. The sun winked off it in the morning. Philip said it was thirty-six feet deep and very dangerous.

Secrets

Kylie was forbidden to lift the lid. It was off-limits. She was fascinated by it. Some afternoons she sat out under the grapevines with her photo album, turning pages and looking across every now and then at that glinting lid. It couldn't be seen from the back verandah; it was obscured by a banana tree and a leaning brick wall.

In all her photographs, there was not one of her father. He had been the photographer in the family; he took photos of Kylie and her mother, Kylie and her friends, but he was always out of the picture, behind the camera. Sometimes she found herself looking for him in the pictures. Sometimes it was a game for her; at others she didn't realise she was doing it.

C Complete this summary of the first part of the story by adding three fairly short sentences. Discuss your ideas first with another student.

> Kylie feels left out from her mother and Philip's activities. She becomes interested in the chickens in the yard. Somehow her secret helps her to feel less lonely. She finds a second egg and then finds out where others are being laid by an unhealthy-looking hen ....
> ....
> ....

Read the second part of the story and listen to it on the cassette.

Part two

Two weeks passed. It was a sunny, quiet time. Ten eggs came to be secreted behind the piece of tin against the back fence. The hen began sitting on them. Kylie suspected something new would happen. She visited the scraggy, white hen every day to see her bright eyes, to smell her musty warmth. It was an important secret now. She sneaked kitchen scraps and canary food up the back each evening and lay awake in bed wondering what would happen.

It was at this time that Kylie began to lift the lid of the well. It was not heavy and it moved easily. Carefully, those mornings, shielded by the banana tree, she peered down into the cylindrical pit which smelt sweaty and dank. Right down at the bottom was something that looked like an engine with pipes leading from it. A narrow, rusty ladder went down the wall of the well. Slugs and spiderwebs clung to it.

One afternoon when Philip and her mother were locked in the big bedroom, laughing and making the bed bark on the boards, Kylie took her photo album outside to the well, opened the lid and with the book stuffed into the waistband of her shorts, went down the ladder with slow, deliberate movements. Flecks of rust came away under her hands and fell whispering a long way down. The ladder quivered. The sky was a blue disc above growing smaller and paler. She climbed down past the engine to the moist sand and sat with her back to the curving wall. She looked up. It was like being a drop of water in a straw or a piece of rice in a blowpipe – the kind boys stung her with at school. She heard the neighbours' rooster crowing, and the sound of the wind. She looked through her album. Pictures of her mother showed her looking away into the distance. Her long, wheaten hair blew in the wind or hung still and beautiful. It had been so long. Her mother never looked at the camera. Kylie saw herself, ugly and short and dark beside her. She grew cold and climbed out of the well.

It seemed a bit of an ordinary thing to have done when she got out. Nevertheless, she went down every day to sit and think or to flick through the album.

The hen sat on her eggs for three weeks. Kylie sat on the fence and gloated, looking into the chookhouse next door at the rooster and his scrabbling hens who did not know what was happening her side of the fence. She knew now that there would be chicks. The encyclopaedia said so.

On nights when Philip and her mother had friends over, Kylie listened from the darkened hallway to their jokes that made no sense. Through the crack between door and jamb she saw them touching each other beneath the table, and she wanted to know – right then – why her father and mother did not live together with her. It was something she was not allowed to know. She went back to her room and looked at the only picture in her album where her smile told her that there was something she knew that the photographer didn't. She couldn't remember what it was; it was a whole year ago. The photo was a shot from way back in kindergarten. She was small, dark-haired, with her hands propping up her face. She held the picture close to her face. It made her confident. It made her think Philip and her mother were stupid. It stopped her from feeling lonely.

Philip caught her down the well on a Sunday afternoon. He had decided to weed the garden at last; she wasn't prepared for it. One moment she was alone with the must, the next, the well was full of Philip's shout. He came down and dragged her out. He hit her. He told her he was buying a padlock in the morning.

That evening the chicks hatched in the space between the sheet of tin and the back fence – ten of them. At dusk, Kylie put them into a cardboard box and dropped them down the well. The hen squawked insanely around the yard, throwing itself about, knocking things over, creating such a frightening noise that Kylie chased it and hit it with a piece of wood and, while it was still stunned, dropped it, too, down the dry well. She slumped down on the lid and began to cry. The back light came on. Philip came out to get her.

Before bed, Kylie took her photograph – the knowing one – from its place in the album, and with a pair of scissors, cut off her head and poked it through a hole in the flyscreen of the window.

D Put these sentences in the right order to produce a summary of the second part of the story.
1. Philip discovers her in the well and hits her.
2. Kylie hits the hen and throws it down the well.
3. Kylie watches the hen sitting on ten eggs.
4. Kylie cuts off her head from the special photo and throws it away.
5. She takes the lid off the well.
6. She starts to go down the well with her photo album every day.
7. She watches Philip and her mother and wonders why her father is not with them.
8. Kylie throws the chicks down the well.
9. She chooses one special photo which makes her feel good.

E Here are some sentences about the three people in this story. Choose one of the verbs, then complete each sentence.

I admire / like / dislike / disapprove of / feel sorry for Kylie because
....
....

I admire / like / dislike / disapprove of / feel sorry for Kylie's mother because ....
....

I admire / like / dislike / disapprove of / feel sorry for Philip because
....
....

In your class, put your sentences together so that you can read them all. Talk about your different responses.

Read the story again.

Secrets

F What do you feel about the story? Talk about it with a partner.

Here is a list of some of the themes in this short story. With your partner, choose the three which you think are most important.

- neglect
- the importance of colours and smells for children
- children's rights
- conflict between different generations
- conflict between men and women
- knowledge as power
- early sexual awareness in children
- coping with the absence of a parent
- the need for security
- coping with feelings of anger
- loneliness
- problems associated with contemporary family life

When you have chosen, write each one on a slip of paper. Put all the papers together, then find out which three were chosen most often by the class. Talk about the reasons for your choices. Does anyone want to add another theme to the list?

Creative development

Here are some further activities for you to choose from.

Completing Kylie's circle diagram

Imagine that you are Kylie. Using the circle diagram on p. 52 again, put crosses on each line to show what Kylie feels. Join the crosses with a pencil line, as you did the first time.

Compare diagrams with other students. Are your patterns similar? Discuss any differences.

Discussing the story's symbols

Some things in this short story seem to have a rather mysterious but powerful symbolic quality. With a few other students, talk about these things.

- the eggs
- the well
- the photos
- Kylie's cutting of the photo

Discuss how you reacted to these items as you read the story. How important do you think they are within the story? Do you feel that they suggest something about Kylie herself?

Discussing children's rights

With another student, decide which of the following rights you agree with, and which you disagree with. Would you add any more?

CHILDREN'S RIGHTS

1 Children have the right not to be hit by parents, guardians or teachers.
2 Children have the right to be told why parents are separating.
3 Children have the right to choose which parent they wish to live with.
4 Children have the right to receive counselling during a family break-up.
5 ....
6 ....

Compare your ideas with those of other students.

Changing Kylie's life

Imagine that you have a magic wand. At a stroke, you can alter one feature of Kylie's life. What would you choose to do? Jot it down.

I would ....
....

Would other students choose to use their magic wand in the same way?

Role-play

Imagine that Kylie has grown up. You meet her and become close friends. She tells you this story from her childhood and wants you to help her to make sense of it. With another student, talk about what you could say to help her understand what she did as a young child.

Act out the conversation between Kylie and yourself.

Dazzler

by Suniti Namjoshi

A Are you an introvert or an extrovert? Fill in this questionnaire to find out.

1. You are planning your holiday – do you choose a crowded, bustling, active holiday resort rather than a quiet, peaceful retreat? Yes / No
2. You are just settling down in comfortable clothes to an evening with a book or the television when some friends pop in unexpectedly. Are you pleased to see them? Yes / No
3. You are planning a party with friends. Would you suggest playing games? Yes / No
4. You are at a dinner party. Your hostess serves up a dish that you think is horrible. Would you refuse to eat it? Yes / No
5. You are spending an evening at your English teacher's house. Suddenly, it is announced that everyone must sing, dance, or tell a story to entertain the others. Would you enjoy doing it? Yes / No
6. Do you feel comfortable when you walk into a room full of people you don't know? Yes / No
7. You are in slow-moving traffic. Do you get frustrated and irritable? Yes / No
8. You arrive just as the lift doors are closing. Would you walk up the stairs rather than wait for the lift? Yes / No
9. Would you prefer an exciting job with few prospects and no pension to a safe job with good prospects and a pension? Yes / No
10. Do you like wearing unusual clothes rather than fashionable clothes? Yes / No
11. Do you usually make your mind up quickly rather than consider each decision thoroughly? Yes / No
12. Someone is boasting to you about their many possessions. Do you try to impress them by talking about all the things you have? Yes / No

Count up the number of 'yes' answers you gave.

Scores:

> If you scored between 8 and 12, you are definitely an extrovert.
> If you scored between 4 and 8, you are neither totally introvert, nor totally extrovert. Your mood and attitude change according to different situations.
> If you scored under 4, you are definitely an introvert.

Show your profile to others in your class, and talk about the situations in the questionnaire. Do you think your own results really show your character?

Students who had a score of 7 and above: make a list of the advantages of being an extrovert.

Students who had a score of 6 or under: make a list of the advantages of being an introvert.

Join other students who made different lists. Take it in turns to read them, or pin them up. Can you think of any disadvantages that counterbalance the advantages listed?

Read the story and listen to it on the cassette.

The sunbird was showing off to such a degree, making the light vibrate off her wingtips, obviously and blatantly singing to herself, that the duck frowned. The sunbird ignored her; she was executing a wholly unnecessary somersault. The duck spoke: 'You ought not to racket and rocket about in quite that manner.' The sunbird was astonished. She stopped in mid-flight and reversed herself. The duck winced – more showing off. 'Why not? It's great fun. Come and try it yourself.' 'You spoil the atmosphere.' The duck was sounding more and more cross. The sunbird by now was bouncing up and down on the end of a twig. 'What, by flying in it?' Suddenly she shot high into the air. The duck felt pacified – she had driven away the nuisance, when the sunbird whizzed past. 'You're a hyperactive headache!' the duck shouted. 'Why? What do I do wrong?' The sunbird was swinging from a nearby creeper. 'You occupy space,' muttered the duck. 'Not as much as you,' retorted the sunbird. The duck lost her temper. With a great flapping of wings she rushed at the sunbird. The sunbird dodged. The duck chased her. At last when the duck was certain that the sunbird had gone, she settled down again to sun herself. Three seconds later she heard the sunbird saying, 'I told you it was fun. Now I'll chase you and you dodge.'

Question: If you were a duck, what would you do?

(a) practise patience
(b) move
(c) start a campaign to make sunbirds illegal
(d) ask the sunbird for flying lessons.

Dazzler

B What are your first impressions of the duck and the sunbird? How many 'yes' answers would the duck give to the questionnaire you filled in? How many would the sunbird? Compare your ideas with other students.

C Look at these two overlapping diagrams.

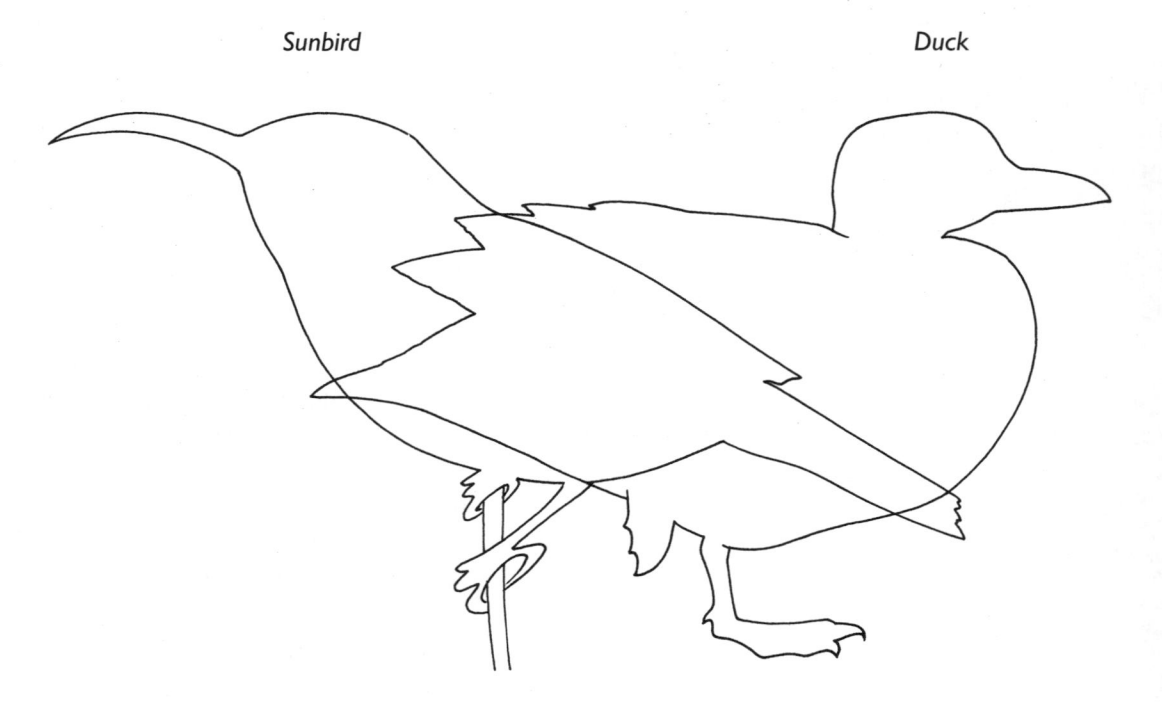

Sunbird   Duck

With a partner, put the following words or expressions into any part of the diagrams that you think is appropriate. Add words or expressions if you wish to. Are these words appropriate for the duck or the sunbird – or both?

sociable   assertive   calm   dominating
introvert   extrovert   mature   intelligent
sensitive   wise   formal   daring   thoughtful
considerate   exciting   impulsive   interesting

(would be a) good colleague   good parent   good boss
good teacher   good musician   good friend   good dancer
good politician

D With a partner, look at these verbs. Use a dictionary or ask others in the class if you don't understand any of them. Which one would be used for which bird, if the story were to continue?

wept   tantalised   groaned   retreated
blustered   whistled   snapped   flashed

E Which do you find more congenial: the duck or the sunbird? Which is more like you? Compare your ideas with others in the class. Are there more sunbirds in the class, or more ducks?

F Which of these statements best expresses your idea of the short story? Discuss each statement with one or two other students and choose one, or write your own.

> The story is about the conflict between introverts and extroverts.
> The story is about different ways of coping with problems in life.
> The story is about decision and indecision, and their results.
> The story is about ....

G With a partner, consider these categories.

Verbs	Adjectives

Put as many words as you can from the story into these categories. Compare your lists with those of other groups. Which one is longer? Together, discuss possible implications of your lists. For example:

> Verbs are usually action words.
> If a text has few verbs, is the effect static or calm?
> If a text has a lot of verbs, is the effect lively? Action-packed?
> What is the effect in this story?
> Adjectives are usually descriptive words. Are there a lot of adjectives in this story? What is the effect?

Creative development

Here are some further activities for you to choose from.

Discussing problem-solving

What kind of a problem-solver are you? When you are faced with a problem, do you

> try patiently to solve it?
> ask advice about what you should do?
> get irritated?
> try to ignore it?
> have another way of dealing with it? ....

Compare your replies with those of others in the class. Can you think of any advantages (or disadvantages) in your problem-solving style?

Answering questions

What is your answer to the final question in the short story 'what would you do if you were a duck?'

In groups, write four choices in answer to the question 'what would you do if you were a sunbird?' Ask another group to choose one of your choices. What are the popular options for sunbirds?

Using alliteration

Alliteration (the repeating of the first sound in a series of words) has a long tradition in English prose and poetry. It is often used to emphasise action or sound words. In this short story, the author uses two amusing alliterative expressions: 'hyperactive headache' and 'racket and rocket'. In small groups, make a list of two or three people whom you know personally, or famous people. Think of one verb or adjective that is typical of each of them. Then add at least one alliterative word to it, to make an expression like the two in the short story.

Read your alliterative phrases to another group, and ask them to guess who is being described.

Discussing show-offs

How is showing off viewed in your society? Are people who show off sometimes admired? Do other people find them irritating? In small groups, describe two situations where showing off might typically take place and how people present would react.

Making choices for a video

Imagine that your group is going to make a video of the short story. Together, decide on

- the screen image that you want to accompany the title of the short story at the beginning of the video.
- the kind of music you want at the beginning, before the narration or action begins.

You may wish to present the story dramatically to the class. A simple way of doing this is to present a mime version accompanied by the narration – with your own images, if you like, and your own music.

Making a puppet version of the story

Make a puppet theatre version of the story for children. Try and perform it for a group of children if possible.

Misunderstood

an anonymous story

A These drawings tell the story of a baboon. They are not in the right order. With another student, study the drawings and put them in an appropriate sequence. Then build up the story together. When you are ready, tell your story to another pair and listen to theirs. How similar are your stories?

Misunderstood

📖 📼 **Read the story for the first time and listen to it on the cassette.**

Misunderstood

This is an older story than most of our others. It dates back, indeed, to the year 1864, when the pet of a British regiment, stationed in Jamaica, was a baboon. He was a meditative

HALF-STRANGLED.

and extremely thoughtful baboon, and his habits and manners provided continual amusement for the officers, before whose mess-room windows his dwelling was placed. He was tethered by a long, light chain, but even with this restraint he managed to get into a

DANDLED AND FONDLED—

Misunderstood

THIS WAY—

good deal of mischief. As, for instance, on one day, when he conceived himself insulted by a certain young officer, and instantly fell to pelting the mess-room windows with such terrific effect that his habitation was removed to a less commanding

THAT WAY—

spot. Here his amusements still went on, however. Any living creature that ventured within his chain-radius was apt to have a busy minute or two, and the unhappy fowls, who often strayed within reach, were grabbed instantly, and sometimes

AND THE OTHER.

Misunderstood

strangled, though he more often amused himself by plucking or half-plucking his unhappy prisoner before releasing it.

One fowl, however, he took a sudden and violent fancy for. He grabbed it, it is true, but he neither plucked it nor wrung its neck, but, instead, dandled and fondled it with such demonstrative affection that quite possibly the unfortunate cock

KILLED BY KINDNESS.

would have preferred plucking. He squeezed it, he stroked it, rubbed it, nursed it, held it aloft and danced it, released it for a moment, and playfully hauled it back by the leg when it made for liberty. The bird did not in any way reciprocate his affection; in fact, altogether misunderstood it. But the baboon persevered, and held firmly on to his pet. He felt confident of winning it over by

MOURNED.

persistent kindness, and since his earlier demonstrations had proved unsuccessful, he renewed them with more vigour. He stroked it the other way, rubbed it more persistently, danced it more quickly, and squeezed it a good deal harder. But even these attentions failed to rouse its affection, and at last, in the midst of an extra-friendly hug, the perverse cock died, misunderstanding the devoted baboon to the last.

Misunderstood

He was overwhelmed with grief. To think that at last, when he had secured a creature he could really love, it should die ere he could induce it fittingly to reciprocate his affection. It was very sad. He set about the last sad rites with every manifestation of sorrow. In solemn grief he buried his departed playmate at the foot of a tall tree, where the grass might grow and the birds sing over its grave. Then he sat him down before the grave and mourned; neglected all his usual amusements, and mourned sorely day by day for a fortnight. But at the end of that time he could bear his grief no longer; so he dug up his departed pet and ATE IT!

A CANNIBAL SAVAGE.

B Complete these sentences.
1 The baboon threw things at the officers' ....
2 The officers moved his ....
3 He caught and sometimes strangled ....
4 However, he showed great .... for one particular fowl.
5 The bird did not .... the baboon.
6 So the baboon .... his displays of affection.
7 Sadly, the bird ....
8 The baboon .... his friend near a tree.
9 He entered a period of solemn ....
10 After two weeks, he could not cope with his feelings and .... up and .... his dead pet.

Is this story noticeably different from the one you created in A?

Misunderstood

Read the story again.

C This story was written in the nineteenth century and its language is of that period. Look at the following rewritten sentences or expressions and decide which of the original lines in the story they represent.

1. One day he felt that he was being made a fool of by one of the officers so he started throwing things at the windows.
2. He had a sudden crush on one of the birds.
3. He gently rocked the fowl with obvious warmth and pleasure.
4. He pulled it back when it tried to get away.
5. Fancy it dying before he could get it to show its true feelings for him!
6. He stopped having his usual fun.

D Did you find the story amusing or sad, or both? Discuss your feelings about it. What would be an alternative title for this story? Discuss some possibilities with other students.

Listen to four people discussing their reactions to the story. What titles do they suggest? Compare them with yours.

Creative development

Here are some further activities for you to choose from.

A debate

One of the themes in the story is that relationships are a source of constant misunderstanding. No matter how hard people try, their intentions may well be misunderstood by others. Organise a debate on the following motion: 'This group believes that misunderstanding amongst people is much more common than understanding.'
Divide the class into groups of three or four people. Each group prepares arguments either for the motion, or against it. Make sure that each side of the argument is equally represented.
Each group then makes a presentation. When they have finished, other groups can ask them questions or challenge what they have said.
At the end of the debate, have a show of hands to see if the motion has been carried or defeated.

Writing a letter

Write a letter to an animal rights group in Jamaica, describing the baboon's current situation, recommending that the baboon be rescued from its current plight and suggesting how its life might be improved.

Misunderstood

Writing the story's moral

Some stories have a moral – a lesson to be learnt from what happens. What, in your view, is the moral of this tale? Write your moral down and then compare it with others.

Discussing the behaviour of animals

The story has a strong anthropomorphic element – that is, the baboon is described as having human-like emotions such as 'affection', 'grief', 'love'. With another student look at this list of feelings that animals may experience. Which of these animals, in your view, actually have these feelings?

grief happiness love suspicion jealousy regret fear ecstasy

Compare your opinions. Is there some measure of agreement?
If you don't believe that animals experience feelings at all, how would you describe the behaviour of pets, for example, who seem so unhappy when their owners die?

Misunderstood

Writing with animal similes

Humans are often compared to animals. Look at the following animals and try to place them in the spaces to form an appropriate expression in English.
Check your answers together.

to laugh like a(n)	....		
as sly as a(n)	....	owl	ox
as quiet as a(n)	....	lion	gazelle
as strong as a(n)	....	mouse	pig
as wise as a(n)	....	wolf	mule
as hungry as a(n)	....	fox	hyena
as graceful as a(n)	....		
as stubborn as a(n)	....		
as fat as a(n)	....		

What other qualities do these animals have that might produce new comparisons? For example, 'as greedy as a pig'; 'as light as a mouse'. With another student create three new expressions. You can use other animals if you prefer.

Write a paragraph about a person, using an animal image in an extended way. Here is an example.

> He had the appetite of a starving wolf. His eyes seemed haunted by hunger, and just as a wolf's nose might twitch when detecting the first scent of a terrified victim, his nostrils fluttered as he smelt the meat sizzling in the kitchen. When the plate eventually came, he pounced and attacked. The meal had no chance of survival.

Shell songs
A letter from the Laird's wife

by George Mackay Brown

A Divide the class into two halves.

ONE HALF
Imagine you are a member of a rich, aristocratic family. You own a large house with large gardens and an estate, near the sea. The family has servants, including gardeners. How would you feel about these situations?

	I'd like it.	It wouldn't bother me.	I'd hate it.
The servants say 'Sir' or 'Madam' every time they speak to you.			
You're often in a big house, alone except for the servants.			
You have a lot of time for reading and going for walks.			
You can give financial help to the poor people on your estate when you feel like it.			
Your life is free from the material pressures that other people feel.			

Shell songs

THE OTHER HALF

Imagine you are a member of a poor family with a tiny piece of land on the estate of a wealthy aristocrat. You have very little money and cannot afford proper treatment when someone in your family is ill. How would you feel about these situations?

	I'd like it.	It wouldn't bother me.	I'd hate it.
You're supposed to say 'Sir' or 'Madam' every time you meet the estate owners.			
You earn your living by your own labour.			
It's hard to put aside money for emergencies.			
You are part of a community – other people are in the same position as you.			
Your situation is stable – you're part of an enduring tradition.			

Share your thoughts with people in your half, and when you are ready, interview someone from the other half to find out how 'the other half lives'.

B The story you are going to read has two central characters – a nine-year-old boy from a poor farming family, and the wife of an estate owner. The story is set on an island in Scotland. What do you think the story might be about? Quickly write down one or two possibilities with another person.

Read the first part of the story and listen to it on the cassette.

Part one

Dearest Alicia,

I must tell you about this strange thing that has happened here.

Do you remember Hundland who used to come and help in the Hall garden sometimes in summer? He is a small man with a brown silky beard and blue eyes. He is a good worker, and quiet in his speech. One thing about him, when James or I speak to him, he will not remove his hat, or say 'sir' and 'ma'am'.

Hundland works a croft on the far side of the island. He is married and has several children.

Three days ago, Tuesday, Hundland had a boy with him, aged nine or ten, when I saw him working in the tulip-beds. This child was wandering slowly here and there about the garden. I could see his lips moving. He nodded from time to time. His hands made slow shapes. He was a very small boy indeed, and not very pretty, with light sand-coloured hair. My first impression was: he is a bit simple in the head.

I opened the window. I called, 'Good morning, Hundland!' The man merely turned his face and nodded. The child fled as if he had been shot, behind the sycamore tree.

'What child is that?' I asked.

Hundland replied, still bent over the blossoms, 'He's Tom. He's our youngest boy. The wife's not well today. I thought I would take him off her hands. He's more trouble, in a way, than all the others.'

'Tom,' I called, 'come from behind the tree. I have an orange and a piece of chocolate for you.'

There was no answer. There was a white five-pointed star stuck to the hither side of the trunk, Tom's hand.

'He won't come out!' said Hundland. 'He's the strangest boy I ever saw. He wouldn't show himself if you were to offer him a piece of gold. I don't know what's to become of the creature when he's grown. He's frightened of boats. He's frightened of horses. He wants to know all about them, all the same. He's frightened of any stranger that comes about. That won't do in a crofter-fisherman. He might grow out of it. He'll have to.'

'Surely he ought to be at school,' I said.

'He's frightened of the teacher, too, and the big boys; they won't leave him alone. He's as ignorant as the scarecrow when it comes to letters and figures. He's upset this morning, because his mother's in bed. The only time he's happy is when he's by himself. He contents himself with the daft games he makes up ...'

These were the words of my radical gardener to me, the most he's ever spoken. (But never a touch to the cap.)

Shell songs

It was a most beautiful morning, Alicia, all blue and gold and green. I decided not to waste the day (James has been all week in Edinburgh on business). I took my book and parasol and cushion and walked along to the beach, which was quite empty, as the fishermen had taken advantage of the weather to set their creels here and there under the cliffs on the west side.

I sat down on a rock and opened my book of Shenstone's poems. Everything was quite beautiful and tranquil. Nature smiled. It was so peaceful I could hear the horse in the field above champing and moving through the grass. I could sense, almost, the earth's juices flowing.

(How is it words in a book are never so beautiful and interesting outside, in the sun? Of course they are, they must be; but books seem made for opening beside a fire indoors, with the yellow waverings of candle-light on the white pages. My friend, I would rather than any book that you had been there to share that beautiful day with me! There is a selfishness in solitary enjoyment.)

It seemed, however, that I was not destined to be solitary for too long. I heard the faintest rhythmic displacement of dry sand-grains. Who could it be, the despoiler of my solitude? I raised the rim of my summer hat, and looked.

It was a small boy, anonymous against the blue and silver glitterings of ocean.

His mouth, between the sea and the fields, was ringing like a little bell.

Dear Alicia, the boy spoke as if the shells and stones and water were living things, and could understand what he was saying. It was the strangest experience: I hidden in my rock cranny, this boy (whoever he was) wandering here and there about the shore, chanting.

I listened, half-amused and half-wonderstruck. Shenstone lay spreadeagled at my feet, the pages slowly curling in the sun.

Should I declare myself? It seemed a shame to break the natural flow of the boy's phantasy. This most strange monologue went on and on. On an impulse, I plucked a pencil from my bag and wrote, as best I could, on the blank pages of *Shenstone's Works*, the words of my shore wanderer. It seemed a shame that only the empty unremembering empyrean should be given such a unique recital.

I cannot convey how fresh and exquisite the words were in that setting. My pencil stumbled on and on, and slowly blunted.

Naturally, I missed much. The boy wandered here and there. Often I could only hear – as it were – an indistinct music. And, then, pencil on paper is tardy, and his words, however indistinct, came with the freshness and urgency of a spring.

C When you have finished, choose one of the main characters, either the Laird's wife or the boy, and make notes about what your chosen character is like or the impressions you get of them.

The Laird's wife is	The boy is
....	....
....	....
....	....
....	....
....	....

Compare your notes with another student's. Have you found different things, or made different interpretations?

Read the second part of the story and listen to it on the cassette.

Part two

Such as I gathered, I send you to marvel at. If they appear in broken lines, my excuse is that they seemed like a scattering of primitive unpolished stones.

Here I go.
I'm writing things in the sand.
I'm writing letters
To a bird and a shell.
I should be writing
On a slate in the school.
      *

The sea will cure her.
I'll take sea
Up to the house in this shell.
'Drink this, Mother.'
      *

I don't think he'll ever die, the Laird
Mr Sweyn.
The lady, she's kind,
She's beautiful and she's sweet
So she'll die.
A pity that, a great pity
For old Mr Sweyn.
      *

Shell songs

        Now, then, I *will* go to school.
        Tomorrow,
        Every day I'll go.
        I'll read the books, hard.
        I'll study.
        I'll go to Edinburgh, the college there.
        I'll be a doctor. I will.
        I'll say to her in the bed,
        'Get well. I'm here. Take this medicine.'
                    *

        I can do anything with you I like,
        Sand.
        I've drawn a cottage.
        There are people living in it.
        They're all singing.
        Look at their round mouths.
        There's a mother
        At a table, with pots and plates.
                    *

        Are you listening, shell?
        You
        Are all whispers and whispers.
        Listen. Tell me
        Where the hidden treasure is, the box
        Full of silver coins.
        Then
        My father will be able to pay his rent.
                    *

        I am Mr Sweyn.
        I live up at the Hall. I do.
        Seagull,
        How do you know I amn't Mr Sweyn?
        I am Mr Sweyn the Laird.
        I say,
        'Miss Ingsetter, you are sacked from the school.'
        Then I say,
        'Mrs Hundland is to stop coughing,
        I have a room for her
        High up, where blue air comes in.'
                    *

Shell songs

Nobody sees me on the shore.
Nobody
Hears, only a shell and a gull.
They are arguing.
The gull says, 'Her face is burning. Then it is grey.
She is very sick.'
The shell sings, 'The mother,
She is never going to die.'
                    *
Once she was sick before.
Then she got up.
She lit the fire, she polished all our boots.
                    *
I'm tired. I'm in trouble. I'm bad. I'm idle.
Shell and gull,
I should be taking the sweat from my mother's face.

There was silence at last, but for the first ebb noises and the cries of a rock-questing gull. It had gotten cold in my rock cranny.

The boy had wandered away.

My hand was numb with writing (as best I could) all those 'native woodnotes wild'.

I looked out. The sands were flushed with the last of the sun.

The boy was a trembling dot against the far reaches of the shore.

I knew – if I had not known already – that it was Tom Hundland.

I had an impulse to cry after him to come back – I would do what I could for his mother and his family.

He heard me. It must have been a thin echo, my cry, at that distance, in the first shadows. He went like a bird up the nearest shore path to the road above.

My hand, dear Alicia, was numb with writing, and with the first chill of evening; and with something more, beyond the plight of that cottage with the skull on the window-sill.

Shell songs

D What do you think of the boy's song? Choose the two ideas that are closest to your own, then compare with other students.

- It's not really a song, just a stream of words and thoughts from a confused child.
- It's a sort of primitive poem.
- It's more powerful than the rest of the letter.
- It shows how lonely the boy is.
- The song reflects the wish to be all-powerful.
- It's a form of communion with nature.
- It doesn't make sense.
- It's a release from tension and stress.

E What do other people think of the Laird's wife? With a partner, choose adjectives and write them in the appropriate place.

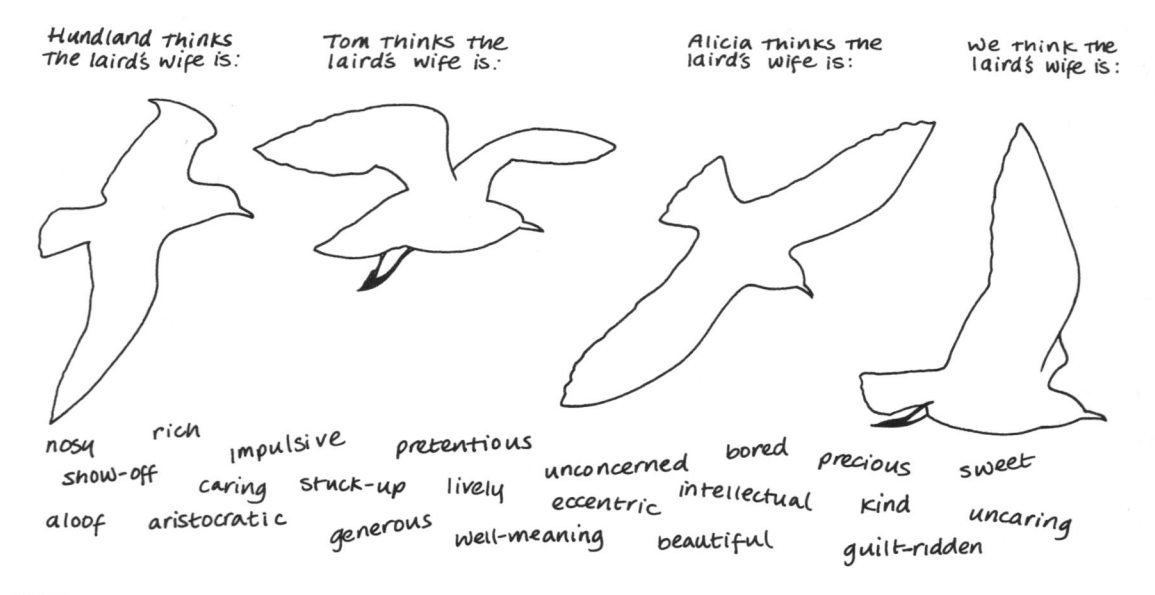

Hundland thinks the laird's wife is:

Tom thinks the laird's wife is:

Alicia thinks the laird's wife is:

We think the laird's wife is:

nosy   rich   impulsive   pretentious   unconcerned   bored   precious   sweet
show-off   caring   stuck-up   lively   eccentric   intellectual   kind   uncaring
aloof   aristocratic   generous   well-meaning   beautiful   guilt-ridden

Read the story again.

F As you read, have a careful look at the language that the writer uses.

The story is in the form of a letter. In the section before the boy's song, can you detect a point after which the woman's style becomes more poetic, more figurative and ornate? Why do you think the style changes?

80

Shell songs

G With a partner, express these phrases from the story in simpler conversational English.

The words in the story	Simpler spoken English
a white five-pointed star	Tom's hand
I heard the faintest rhythmic displacement of dry sand-grains	
Who could it be, the despoiler of my solitude?	
I hidden in my rock cranny	
Shenstone lay spreadeagled at my feet	
shore wanderer	
empty unremembering empyrean	
pencil on paper is tardy	
cries of a rock-questing gull	
The sands were flushed with the last of the sun	

Creative development

Here are some further activities for you to choose from.

Comparing reactions

In groups of three or four compare your ideas on these questions.
    Which part of the story is easier to remember – the boy's song or the woman's letter? Why?
    Which part of the story is the more powerful, in your view?
    Which character makes the strongest impression on your memory?

Supporting reactions from the text

What does the story make you feel? Can you find lines in the story to support one or two of these possibilities?
    sympathy for the boy
    a sense of the atmosphere of a deserted beach
    indignation for the Hundland family's plight
    contempt for a society with such gulfs between rich and poor
    admiration for the poetic language
    intrigued by the boy
    unmoved by the whole story

Shell songs

Writing a letter

Imagine you are Alicia. Write a letter of reply to the Laird's wife.

Imagining the setting

In small groups, using your knowledge and imagination, try to give as many details as you can about one of these.

- What the Laird's Hall looks like inside – furniture, things on the wall, food in the kitchens, pets …
- What the Hundlands' cottage is like – furniture, things on the wall or on the tables, food, animals …

Improvising

Improvise a scene in which the Laird's wife goes to the Hundlands' cottage to offer some money.

Consider these questions in order to imagine the scene more clearly.

How would the Laird's wife approach the subject of a gift of money?
Would the Hundlands act politely, coldly, deferentially?
Would the Hundland family be too proud to accept charity?

Comparing two stories

Both 'Shell songs' and 'The star' are set in Scotland. Both have small boys as key characters. Read or re-read 'The star' and draw up a chart of similarities and differences between Cameron and Tom.

	Similarities	Differences
Tom Hundland		
Cameron		

Which of the two stories did you like best and why?

The authors of the stories

George Mackay Brown (1921 –   )
('Shell songs')

George Mackay Brown lives in Stromness, in the Orkney islands, where he was born. His poems and novels spring from his life in the islands as well as from his feeling for that landscape and for the people who live in it.

Peter Carey (1943 –   )
('Report on the shadow industry')

Peter Carey was born near Melbourne, Australia. He worked in advertising in Sydney and has lived in Queensland, London and New York. He has written both novels and short stories. His work is characterised by its mixture of strong realism and extraordinary fantasy.

Leonora Carrington (1917 –   )
('The debutante')

Born in Lancashire, Leonora Carrington studied art in London. In 1937 she met Max Ernst, settled in Paris with him and exhibited with the Surrealist group. From 1939 she began to publish stories which mingle a strong Surrealist fantasy element with some social comment. Her paintings of strange insect-like humanoids made her internationally famous. She lives in the United States and Mexico.

Alasdair Gray (1934 –   )
('The star')

Alasdair Gray was born in Glasgow, where he still lives. He is also an artist, and worked as an illustrator before turning to fiction in his forties. He has published several novels and a collection of short stories.

Barbara L. Greenberg (1932 –   )
('Important things')

Barbara L. Greenberg was born in Boston, Massachusetts, the state in which she still lives. She has taught on both college and graduate level creative writing programmes. She has published both poetry and short stories.

The authors of the stories

Suniti Namjoshi (1941 –   )
('Dazzler')

Suniti Namjoshi was born in India. She has worked as an Officer in the Indian Administrative Service and in academic posts in India and Canada. Since 1972 she has taught in the Department of English of the University of Toronto and has recently spent time living and writing in Devon. She has published numerous poems, fables, articles and reviews in India, Canada, the United States and Britain.

Alexander McCall Smith (1948 –   )
('Strange animal')

Born and brought up in Zimbabwe, Alexander McCall Smith collected the stories in *Children of Wax* by visiting and recording people, especially elderly people, in Matabeleland. He has translated and adapted the stories from the original Ndebele language.

Malachi Whitaker (1895 – 1975)
('Hannah')

Malachi Whitaker was born in Bradford, Yorkshire. She grew up among books – her father was a bookbinder – and started to write herself when she was very young. However, she was always very self-critical and published only four volumes of short stories and one novel, *And so did I* (1939). After this she stopped writing for publication and her works were largely forgotten until being rediscovered recently.

William Carlos Williams (1883 – 1963)
('Verbal transcription – 6 a.m.')

Born in New Jersey in the United States, William Carlos Williams went to school in France and Switzerland before studying medicine at the University of Pennsylvania. He practised as a doctor in Rutherford. He is best known as a poet and especially for his epic poem *Paterson*.

Tim Winton (1960 –   )
('Secrets')

Born in Perth, Western Australia, he has written several novels and numerous stories. He lives in a small town on the west coast of Australia. He is considered to be one of Australia's most talented young writers.

Notes on the stories

The star

A story set in a working class area of Scotland. A young boy's apparently humdrum life is magically transformed by a 'star' which offers him a dramatic, scintillating escape. The story's poignancy lies in the vivid contrast set up between the boy's lonely, constrained life and the boundless freedom he senses in the world beyond.

Vocabulary and cultural references

There are some Scottish expressions, consisting mainly of representations of the spoken accent:

A'm gawn out – I'm going out
See you're no long then – Make sure you're not out too long
I cannae, sir – I can't, sir

Other expressions which might be a little unusual or which represent Scottish variants on the usual English meaning:

tenement – in Scotland, a large house let in sections to a number of tenants
pulley – a frame from which wet clothes in the house can be raised and lowered by means of a rope
lobby – hallway, passageway, corridor
stairhead – the level space at the top of a flight of stairs (The Scots pronunciation of the second syllable as /hiːd/ and not /hed/ can be heard on the cassette)
midden – a little rubbish heap
lattice – a criss-cross pattern

Strange animal

A gentle folk tale from Africa which has the traditional element of magic, but also makes shrewd observations about the complexity of family relationships.

Vocabulary and cultural references

The vocabulary raises no particular difficulties, and the story line is strong enough to carry the reader over any unknown words.

For non-African readers, the exotic cultural setting constitutes one of the pleasures of this story. Activity H (p. 13) is designed to help learners think about its cultural implications and draw comparisons with their own culture.

Notes on the stories

Hannah

A story whose details vividly recreate a young woman's entry into adulthood in provincial England between the two world wars. In the first part, a portrait of happy expectations and a comfortable standard of living is built up, with hints of the subtle pressures exerted by social convention. The surprise time shift in the second half provides a strong counterpoint, creating a pervasive sense of regret and lost opportunities.

Vocabulary and cultural references

> *dresser* – a sideboard or shelves for plates
> *Sunday-school* classes for religious instruction given at church on Sundays
> *trifle* – a traditional English dessert, consisting of sherry-soaked cake with jam or fruit, covered with custard and cream
> *bodice* – the upper part of a woman's dress
> *rebukingly* – in a way that is meant to reprimand or scold
> *gnarled* – twisted
> *plait* – a length of hair interwoven or braided

Report on the shadow industry

An unusual and mysterious story that haunts the imagination. 'Shadows' dominate the lives of the characters, but the tantalised reader is left wondering about their substance and their meaning. Although the time setting and the location are both uncertain, there are recognisable elements of a modern technological society. The story resists any single, simple interpretation – re-reading and discussion can lead to new perspectives and prove truly rewarding.

Vocabulary and cultural references

Section 1

> *springing up* – being built rapidly
> *Muzak* – the bland background music heard in many Western supermarkets, restaurants, banks, etc.
> *it gives me the shits* – (slang) it frightens me
> *try their luck* – to gamble (usually connected with placing bets)
> *fake evidence* – a proof that is false, designed to deceive people
> *carcinogenic chemicals* – substances that produce cancer
> *apocalypse* – a vision of the future (bringing a dreadful global disaster)

Section 2

> *Bureau of Statistics* – in many countries, a department that collects and publishes facts and statistics about life in that country. The language in this section parodies the language of official reports from the Bureau of

Statistics: use of passives (*are packaged*, *has been explained*) and statistical terms (*percentage increases as ... decreases, direct statistical correlation*)

Section 3

the lottery – a gambling scheme set up by many states
make capital of – to use for one's own profit (here, psychological profit)

Section 5

ambivalent – having mixed and conflicting emotions about something
elusive – difficult to catch

Verbal transcription – 6 a.m.

A story in the form of a monologue: the speech that occupies a slice of time during a doctor's house call. One of the main features is the juxtaposition of everyday concerns and the emergency situation. A strong sense of character and setting is developed with surprisingly few words.

Vocabulary and cultural references

the old reliable – (colloquial) something that works every time
as if we were living on Third Avenue – many cities in America, New York for example, use a numbering system for streets. Third Avenue hints at a wealthy area
blue-jay – usually a wild bird rather than a domestic one
pajamas – (US spelling) pyjamas, nightwear
needles – in this case, for giving an injection

The debutante

This is a shocking story, with bizarre images and a rather blood-curdling mixture of reality and fantasy. A main theme is the existence of 'bestial' instincts just below the veneer of polite social ritual. Part of its power derives from the fact that the horror is treated in a matter-of-fact way, parodying the cold, unthinking cruelty of the social milieu. The story thus becomes a brutal indictment of upper-class values.

The first reading of 'The debutante' can sometimes be unsettling or even distressing. Our warm-up activities provide some kind of preliminary awareness by focusing upon the story's historical context, emphasising parallels in the artistic movements of the period. In our experience, this helps readers to distance themselves from the story's shocking elements while gaining further insights into its aesthetic objectives.

Similarly, one of the creative development activities, a listening task based on a biographical sketch of the author, is included to further broaden the context within which the story can be viewed.

Although English by birth, Leonora Carrington wrote in French. The text given here is her own translation from the original French.

Vocabulary and cultural references

debutante – until the 1960s, young women from wealthy families in England were presented at the Monarch's Court and at special balls when they reached adulthood and were therefore considered of marriageable age. Activity C (p. 39) provides learners with some cultural background about this practice. If learners already have this knowledge, the activity can be omitted.

bloody nuisance – a colloquial and (for a debutante) rather vulgar expression of annoyance (would she use it in front of her mother?)

make small talk – have a social conversation on banal themes

fleurs-de-lis – flowers with three petals, used in heraldry to denote royalty or the aristocracy

in tip-top form – very well (in register, colloquial, upper-class, though used in this case by the hyena)

Gulliver's Travels – a pertinent reference – this classic eighteenth-century novel, with its strange lands and bizarre human or animal characters, satirises the English society of its day

Important things

A very short story that generates a surprising amount of tension. It has a universal theme, the struggle between parents and children, as children grow up and become at once more demanding and more independent.

Vocabulary and cultural references

whimpered – whined, asked in a plaintive way, as small children do
tugged – pulled insistently (at clothing, for example)
ingenuous – innocent (here, pretending not to know)
mind their manners – (colloquial) be more polite
relief from pain – an end to pain
fudge cake with chocolate frosting – an American treat for children, a cake coated with a sugary chocolate topping
resort to – do something as a last step when everything else has failed

The story has a number of sayings which are well known, or which encapsulate traditional wisdom: *the dawn will follow the dark* implies that life will go on; *every dog will have its day* implies that everyone gets something out of life. *The Littlest Soldier* is a traditional story whose moral is that good behaviour will be rewarded.

Notes on the stories

Secrets

This contemporary Australian story focuses on the ways in which a child tries to come to terms with the traumas of family breakdown. It evokes in a rather disturbing way the child's feelings of isolation and powerlessness, which make her transfer her emotions onto the things around her.

Vocabulary and cultural references

Some words reflect the Australian setting, the new house with its *loungeroom* (sitting room), *yard* (garden), *picket fence* (fence made of wooden posts), *bore well* (deep hole drilled for water) with its *galvanized tin cover* and the next door house with its *wired-up run* (a space for the chickens, surrounded by a wire fence) and its *chookhouse* (henhouse).

> *pasties* – pastry filled with meat or vegetables
> *crabbed* – went round exploring
> *fossicking* – (Australian) searching for
> *off-limits* – a place that is forbidden
> *musty* – smelling old, stale
> *cylindrical pit* – a deep round hole
> *must* – mould, mildew – a growth caused by damp
> *padlock* – a detachable lock

Dazzler

A very short story which quickly establishes sharp tensions between the irrepressible, energetic displays of one character and the simmering impatience of the other. The effects are fashioned with great economy yet the story has the visual and symbolic power characteristic of fables and folk tales. The amusing form of the ending suddenly transports the story into contemporary times.

Vocabulary and cultural references

> *sunbird* – brightly coloured small songbird found in tropical regions, especially in Africa
> *to show off* – to behave in a way that invites attention and admiration
> *blatantly* – visibly, obviously (in this context, singing loudly to make sure she is heard)
> *to racket and rocket about* – to fly around with great speed while at the same time making a lot of noise
> *winced* – made a sudden movement in painful reaction
> *whizzed* – flew rapidly making a 'whizzing' sound
> *hyperactive* – abnormally active
> *hyperactive headache* – a nuisance caused by someone being overactive
> *a creeper* – a plant that creeps along the ground or climbs trees or walls

Notes on the stories

Misunderstood

Unlike the other ten stories, this illustrated tale was first published anonymously in the nineteenth century. The language is of that period, but need not present major problems as the plot and context are clear enough to carry the reader along. The story highlights the tragic consequence of failure to communicate but it also raises interesting questions about the worlds of animals and humans.

Vocabulary and cultural references

The paraphrasing activity (C, p. 70) provides some help with possible language difficulties.

> *regiment* – a unit of the army
> *mess-room* – (military) dining-room
> *demonstrative* – showy, visible
> *plucking* – pulling out feathers
> *dandled, fondled, squeezed, stroked, rubbed, nursed, danced* – all the physical ways in which the baboon shows his affection (shown in the illustrations)
> *last rites* – ceremonies for the dead

Shell songs

An atmospheric tale, in the form of a letter, which captures the wildness and isolation of the Scottish coast. The story is structured around a series of contrasts: the shy crofter's son and the wife of a wealthy landowner; the preciosity of her literary leanings and the spontaneity of the boy's wistful chant; leisure and toil; wealth and poverty; sickness and health.

Vocabulary and cultural references

The story's setting is a wealthy estate and shows both a poor family who work on it and the landowner's wife. The cultural implications of this situation are explored in Activity A (pp. 73-74).

Some of the difficulties presented by the flowery language of the Laird's wife's letter are dealt with in Activity F (p. 80).

> *Laird* – (Scotland) owner of a large estate
> *hall* – a large house or mansion
> *croft* – (Scotland) a small farm
> *simple in the head* – lacking intelligence
> *scarecrow* – an object in the shape of a person set in the fields to frighten away the birds
> *daft* – foolish, mad
> *radical* – favouring fundamental changes in social institutions (the gardener is seen as rather revolutionary because he won't remove his hat!)

creels – (Scotland) a trap for catching lobsters, etc.
champing – munching, chewing or biting
plight – a situation of hardship, difficulty

The boy in his song uses the Scottish form: *amn't* (am not).
The Laird's wife uses the Scottish form: *gotten* (also used in American English).

Key

The star

G

Words/expressions which indicate poverty: *the lobby/stairhead* (indicating a tenement flat); *three flights* (the family lives three floors up); *cold; coldly lit stairs; he slept with his brother.*

Words/expressions which indicate the rich new world of the star: *warm; ruby glow; white and blue; cave in an iceberg; pattern of a snow-flake; the grandest thing he had ever seen; an ocean of glittering blue-black waves under a sky full of huge galaxies; the sound in a sea-shell; flower, jewel, moon or landscape; gentle warmth in his pocket; cool green pupil.*

Report on the shadow industry

C

1 It is implied that this is true   2 T   3 F (the smoke is of different, brilliant colours)   4 T (to the narrator's country at very least)   5 T   6 T   7 F   8 T   9 F   10 F   11 T   12 T

Important things

C

1 Whimper and tug, stand eye to eye and show their teeth.
2 (Not stated, but the children keep on asking, so they are not satisfied.)
3 They say there are better words than those used by the parent (implying they already have more knowledge about it).
4 They say they are already carrying out that advice and when the parent continues, they laugh at the parent.
5 (Not stated, but the children keep on asking, so they are not satisfied.)
6 (Not stated, but the children keep on asking, so they are not satisfied.)
8 The children continue to ask their question.
9 They ask when and are unimpressed when told that this will happen some day.
10 They already knew it and become impatient with the parent.

Key

Creative development – Dialogue writing with proverbs

Every dog will have its day.
Pride goes before a fall.
Every cloud has a silver lining.
A rolling stone gathers no moss.
Least said soonest mended.
Look before you leap.
Patience is a virtue
Ignorance is bliss.
Marry in haste repent at leisure.
A bird in the hand is worth two in the bush

Secrets

B
Philip; father; yard; warm; secret.

D
7 9 3 5 6 1 8 2 4

Misunderstood

A
3 6 2 7 5 1 4

B
1 mess-room windows   2 habitation   3 fowls that came within his reach
4 affection   5 respond to, reciprocate the affection of   6 renewed, redoubled   7 died   8 buried   9 mourning   10 dug; ate.

C
1 … on one day, when he conceived himself insulted by a certain young officer, and instantly fell to pelting the mess-room windows …
2 One fowl, however, he took a sudden and violent fancy for.
3 … dandled and fondled it with such demonstrative affection …
4 … playfully hauled it back by the leg when it made for liberty.
5 To think that … it should die ere he could induce it fittingly to reciprocate his affection.
6 … neglected all his usual amusements …

Creative development – Writing with animal similes

These similes are current in English: to laugh like a hyena   as sly as a fox
as quiet as a mouse   as strong as an ox   as wise as an owl   as hungry as
a lion (possibly a wolf)   as graceful as a gazelle   as stubborn as a mule
as fat as a pig

Tapescripts

Hannah

A Remembering a party

Try to remember a party you went to either recently or some time ago. It might be a birthday party, or some family celebration, or a wedding.

Were you looking forward to it before the party? Were you excited? Did you think about the people you might meet there? Did you think about the clothes you were going to wear?

You're now at the party again. Look around. Are you inside or outside? What is the place like? Are there any special decorations for the party?

Walk around. Who can you see? Are they friends? Strangers? Family? Is everyone there of the same age? What sort of clothes are people wearing? What are you wearing? Are the clothes comfortable? Bright colours?

What is there to eat and drink?

Who do you talk to? Do you spend a lot of time talking to one person, or do you move around? Is there someone there you notice more than the others?

Are you happy at this party or uneasy?

The debutante

Creative development – Guessing and finding out about the author

Leonora Carrington's life

Leonora Carrington was born in 1917, the daughter of a wealthy English clothing manufacturer and an Irish mother. She spent her childhood in a mansion in the North of England and was educated at convent schools until she went to Florence in Italy to be 'finished' at Miss Penrose's Academy. Her parents gave her a glamorous ball at the Ritz, a splendid hotel in London, and she was presented at Court to King George V. But instead of getting married and settling for a life of 'prosperous tedium', she was determined to become a painter. She went to art school in the same year as the very first Surrealist exhibition in London. Soon afterwards she met Max Ernst, an important Surrealist painter. They ran away together although he was already married and 27 years older than she was. They lived in Paris and the South of France. When Ernst was put in prison at the start of the Second World War, she became depressed and ended up in a mental hospital in Madrid. She was rescued by her nanny who travelled to Spain in a submarine. She met a Mexican diplomat in Lisbon, married him and went to live in New York. Her second husband was a Hungarian photographer and they lived for a long time in Mexico City and had two sons. A woman of many talents, she combined writing, painting and design for the theatre.

Misunderstood

D Some reactions to the story

A: I think it's a delightful story. I think the, probably the title is 'Don't eat the ones you love'.

B: Unless they're dead, or what?

A: Check the sell by date. No, it's lovely, it's erm ... I kept finding myself worrying about the moment ... as after this point had passed in the story it kept lingering in my mind of why this baboon had gone off in ... and thrown things at the soldier who was mimicking him and then everything else that followed, that seemed to have been a turning point in his life, you know, so it seems to be a major point in the story. But it was fun – lovely story.

C: I felt sad because here's this poor baboon – it wasn't his choice and he was brought there and kept there as a pet and then he was mimicked by the officer, and then, as he became more angry, the officer mimicked him even more and then, as if to punish him for throwing things at the other officers, he was taken away to the bottom of the garden and the whole story is too sad for words. I think I should call it 'Dear departed'.

B: 'Dear departed'. 'Dear departed' that's a ... ee ... oh. I felt sorry for the baboon, but then I felt sorry for the hen, I mean, you know ... very ... it's ... bizarre eating of ... at the end, eating the hen. I ...

D: What do you think it would be called?

B: Boy, that's a ... I don't know, that's a real poser. There's a ... it's definitely a *Twilight zone* episode.

D: Uh-huh. I think it would be 'Confessions of a military mascot'.

C: Oh, wonderful.

B: That's a great title, that's a great title.

D: I felt so upset about the baboon being rejected to the bottom of the garden ...

B: Yes.

D: ... it completely threw me when I first read it as ... really was getting upset about the poor chap.

C: Aren't baboons vegetarian?

D: He ate it out of love, I think this, yes ... to get closer ...

A: ... I enjoyed the story, but I did find it sad in the sense of what happens to it, but somehow after that turning point that I mentioned earlier it seemed that ever... it concentrated on, on the baboon trying to deal with being locked up and ... and reconstitute himself and get back together again ...

B: Right, right.
A: … and have some control over his life and show affection which was so sorely missing from the soldiers and so on, but it … it's rather sad that the … he tried to show it to another species, as it were, and this other species wouldn't deal with it, so there are all sorts of social messages in …
D: Æsop's fable sort of line of it, I was … oh, what's going to come next?, oh, what's going to be the actual moral of this tale?
B: So what is the moral of this tale?
C: In a way it, er, pinpoints man's inhu… inhumanities to animals, you know, we … we really are quite cruel to the animals and, in fact, the … it was the officer's cruelty to the animal that changed its behaviour.
D: I love the … the sentence in it after he tried stroking the hen that he liked so much, so he stroked it the other way … and you get these gorgeous feathers being pulled away.
A: Yeah, I suppose there's another layer in there of how do you deal with affection which is so overwhelming, I mean they … they ostracised this baboon and turned it into something they didn't know how to deal with … because his own affection to the soldiers had been misused, er … and they'd ostracised him, he didn't know how to temper his own love or need for affection with other people … it's another point, really, that can happen socially.
C: And talking about love here, you're killing with kindness, this is what the baboon did to the poor hen – killed it with kindness.
D: … it's a mice and men, really, isn't it?

To the teacher

The eleven stories in this anthology have been chosen for their interest and also because they are quite short. This makes them less daunting for learners of English, and more manageable for teachers on a wide variety of courses. They embody universal themes (for example, conflict between the generations) which it is hoped will ensure that their appeal is wide enough for learners to read them with pleasure and motivation. The selection reflects a desire to represent the international flavour of contemporary writing in English.

Level

The stories are likely to appeal to adult or young adult learners of English, at an intermediate to advanced level. There is no specific grading or progression throughout the book, so that teachers can make their own selection according to the level and interests of particular classes. Different stories present different challenges: some are linguistically demanding, some are conceptually demanding in the sense that they say a lot in a very compressed space, some require a leap of the imagination. We have found that most of them make a strong impact on first reading, but that re-reading them brings rewards of new insights and deeper understanding.

Some of the longer or more complex stories are divided into two parts, often with predicting activities to maintain interest and curiosity. The five original parts of 'Report on the shadow industry' are divided into four sections, but in this case the complete story is also available as an unbroken text. Although approaching a text in short sections can help learners with any lexical or cultural difficulties they might have, it does not so closely replicate the experience that readers usually have, of coming to terms with and enjoying a text from start to finish. Teachers will therefore probably wish to make a choice, according to the level of their class: either presenting the story in sections where they judge this to be appropriate, or perhaps with more advanced learners, moving directly from the warm-up to a reading of the whole story.

Warm-up

The activity that precedes reading is crucial. If a central theme is introduced in a way that arouses the interest of the class, and if learners are encouraged to explore what they think and feel about it, then it is much more likely that they will actually want to read the story when they come to it. Warm-up activities are thus designed to put learners directly into the situation that will be encountered in the text, familiarise them if necessary with some of the language needed to discuss it, and above all elicit their own reactions and opinions about it. In some cases, a warm-up might take up a substantial part of the class period – but the rewards it offers, in terms of valuable fluency work, personalisation of the text and motivation, are well worth the time and effort involved.

Warm-up activities can obviously be modified for different learners. Quite often, the teacher may wish to introduce the theme and work through the first activity before turning to the book. For example, before reading 'Important things', learners are asked to consider what a parent should tell children, and when. The book lists a few items as prompts, but teachers might prefer to begin simply by asking the class what they think, and writing up all their suggestions on the board. Students might then be interested to compare their own ideas with those in the book before going on to the group work, where they place each item within one of the age ranges suggested. In this as in so many of the activities, the teacher's enthusiasm and involvement are important ingredients in setting the scene for the story itself.

Choice of activities

The activities that follow reading part or all of a story for the first time are intended either to accompany a first reading (and/or listening) or to prompt re-reading. Their purpose is to get learners to go back to the text, reassess their first impressions, and in so doing deepen their understanding and appreciation of the entire work. We have tried to avoid the kind of conventional 'comprehension questions' which are so often mechanical and demotivating. Instead, we have opted for 'comprehension activities', allowing learners to find out more about the text by themselves rather than being told. These activities often incorporate a puzzle or game element, and will, we hope, prove intriguing enough for learners to derive some pleasure from doing them. There are also tasks which take learners beyond a first understanding of the text, to extend their awareness of some of the underlying issues raised by the stories.

Asking learners to write their own comprehension questions for each other to answer is another strategy teachers can use to make comprehension work more reader-centred.

Whether or not a class works through some part or all of the activities is a decision that only the teacher can make. In some cases, working through them all might be too much. Some classes may need to do more work than others to ensure that they can enjoy and appreciate the story. In the majority of cases, a judicious choice of tasks best suited to the needs or interests of particular learners will prove most satisfactory.

Creative development activities

The same is true of the *creative development* activities. With each story the book offers varied possibilities, some referring back to the text and encouraging further discussion of it, some branching out from the story or its theme into different types of creative work: writing, role-play, discussion or drama activities. We hope that teachers will find one or two amongst these which will appeal to their particular learners. In some classes, groups of students might like to consider the various options and

To the teacher

make a choice themselves. This gives an excellent opportunity for feedback afterwards: groups that have chosen different activities can compare what they have done with some degree of curiosity and interest. It may also be interesting for the class to have an exhibition or poster display of the writing or visuals produced during their *creative development* activities.

Language difficulties

Here again, much is left to the discretion of teachers: they are best placed to know what words or expressions might present problems to their students. In the *Notes on the stories* there are glosses for possible vocabulary or cultural difficulties, but the decision as to how much these have to be pre-taught or highlighted must obviously remain with the teacher.

Our own preference in teaching is to try to encourage learners to read for the main points, especially in their first reading, and not worry unduly about unknown words or expressions. If anything proves really troublesome, it can often be cleared up quite easily by the teacher as she or he goes around the groups, monitoring and helping with their work.

One of the benefits of using fiction, with its vivid imaginative patterns and its appeal to the emotions, is that learners find that they can indeed get a lot from a text even if they do not understand every single word. To reinforce this point, we have included few exercises dealing with specific linguistic points, our aim being to take the learner's attention away from potential textual difficulties and concentrate instead on overall comprehension and enjoyment.

The role of the cassette

Each of the eleven stories in this book is accompanied by a recorded version on cassette. There is a range of ways in which the cassette can be put to good use. Here are a few suggestions.

- Some stories can be listened to rather than read after the warm-up activity. This may be especially appropriate for the very short stories in the anthology, such as 'Important things', 'Dazzler', 'Verbal transcription – 6 a.m'. The story can then be read as the second encounter with the text.
- As each story's activities includes a 'second reading' section, this could be carried out as a listening, if the group of learners is sufficiently confident and proficient. Teachers can then also decide whether that listening should be accompanied by the text, or without the text.
- Although it may not assist conventional reading skills, the option always exists for teachers to use the cassette as an accompaniment to all readings of the stories. Timing will become an important consideration for this particular option.
- Some of the stories in this anthology integrate reading and listening as part of the progression through the story, for example, 'Hannah', 'Secrets', 'Shell songs'. Any of the stories that are presented for reading in sections can alternate between text and listening where that

To the teacher

additional option is appropriate for both learners and the understanding and appreciation of the story.
- If learner interest is sufficient, listening to the cassette can be offered as a final activity in class, after a full progression of reading and response activities has been carried out. Listening at this point should be relaxing and pleasurable.
- Finally, learners can be encouraged to listen to the stories in their own time, on a self-access basis. Frequent returns to the stories in the form of either re-reading or listening can only enhance learners' appreciation of them. It may also build learners' level of confidence and comfort with literature, thus stimulating reading of other unabridged works in English.

General points

It may be worth remembering that it can take a good reader a surprisingly long time to read a story aloud on to a cassette. Teachers might like to assess the time it will take to listen to particular recordings of the complete stories in class, and plan their lessons accordingly.

It is always preferable to use the recordings of stories with a cassette recorder that carries a counter. This enables much more efficient referencing when using rewind to particular sections a second time.

The voices reading the stories represent a range of accents which suit the settings of particular stores and add an appropriate atmosphere. Many learners, however, may not be able to discriminate differences of accent, so it may be unwise to focus on this feature of the recordings.

Thank you

The authors owe an enormous debt to the hundreds of teachers all over the world who have worked with us, helping us to explore and refine our ideas. So often during the course of workshops suggestions were made which surprised and delighted us. Our faith in the value of collaborative effort was more than confirmed. Group work really does throw up precious new insights, for us as well as for our learners!

Our thanks in particular to teachers at IATEFL, TEAL in Vancouver, British Council courses in Chester and at the Middle East Technical University in Ankara, the British Institute in Paris, TEA seminars in the Canary Islands, and many workshops in Spain and Italy.

To all these teachers, and to new readers, we send our best wishes. We hope you enjoy using this book with your classes. If you have any comments to make about it, we would be very happy to hear from you. Write to us in the care of our publisher:

ELT Department
Cambridge University Press
The Edinburgh Building
Shaftesbury Road
Cambridge CB2 2RU
England

Bibliography

Alasdair Gray, 'The star', *Unlikely Stories, Mostly* by Alasdair Gray, Penguin, 1984.

Alexander McCall Smith, 'Strange animal', *Children of Wax* by Alexander McCall Smith, Canongate, 1989.

Malachi Whitaker, 'Hannah', *The Crystal Fountain and Other Stories* by Malachi Whitaker, Paladin, 1984.

Peter Carey, 'Report on the shadow industry', *The Fat Man in History* by Peter Carey, University of Queensland Press, 1974.

William Carlos Williams, 'Verbal transcription – 6 a.m.', *The Doctor Stories*, by William Carlos Williams, New Directions Publishing Corporation, 1984.

Leonora Carrington, 'The debutante', *The House of Fear* by Leonora Carrington, Virago Press, 1989.

Barbara L. Greenberg, 'Important things', *Sudden Fiction, American Short-Short Stories*, ed. R. Shepard and J. Thomas, Penguin, 1988.

Tim Winton, 'Secrets', *Scission* by Tim Winton, McPhee Gribble, 1988.

Suniti Namjoshi, 'Dazzler', *The Blue Donkey Fables* by Suniti Namjoshi, The Women's Press, 1988.

'Misunderstood', anonymous, *The Strand Magazine*, 1896.

George Mackay Brown, 'Shell songs', *Scottish Short Stories*, Introduction by Anne Smith, Collins, 1984.